EVERYDAY FAVORITES
AIR FRYER COOKBOOK

Southwest Burgers, page 124

EVERYDAY FAVORITES
AIR FRYER
COOKBOOK

115 RECIPES MADE EASIER AND HEALTHIER

Linda Larsen

Photography by Tom Story

ROCKRIDGE PRESS

For general information on our other products and services or to obtain technical support, please contact our Customer Care Department within the United States at (866) 744-2665, or outside the United States at (510) 253-0500.

Interior and Cover Designer: Jamison Spittler
Art Producer: Karen Williams
Editor: Justin Hartung
Production Manager: Jose Olivera
Production Editor: Melissa Edeburn

Photography © 2020 Tom Story. Food styling by Karen Shinto.

Cover photo: Garlicky Green Beans, Curly Fries, and Parmesan Chicken Tenders

ISBN: Print 978-1-64739-293-2
eBook 978-1-64739-294-9

R0

I DEDICATE THIS BOOK TO

my dear husband, Doug,

my beautiful nieces, Maddie and Grace,

and my wonderful nephew, Michael.

They are a joy and a delight.

Raspberry-Stuffed French Toast, page 22

CONTENTS

INTRODUCTION

When I bought my first air fryer, I used it to make the kinds of dishes you might expect—perfect French fries and the most fabulous Curried Chicken Nuggets (page 103). In 2016, as I researched and wrote my first air fryer cookbook, I came to appreciate the versatility of this appliance. I found that cookies, cakes, muffins, brownies, stir-fries, casseroles, burgers, meat loaves, kebabs, pizzas, and meatballs are all possible in the air fryer. What a revelation.

The air fryer not only fries foods to crispy perfection, it also bakes, roasts, grills, stir-fries, dehydrates, and rewarms leftovers. Anything an oven, grill, or stovetop can do, the air fryer can do, too—only more quickly and easily. With my air fryer, I can bake apple muffins in 15 minutes, compared to 20 minutes in the oven, which also has to preheat. Think of the air fryer as a small convection oven; the hot, moving air helps the sugars caramelize and leads to a crisp crust and tender interior. Instead of starting my charcoal grill (with all the mess and fuss), waiting 20 minutes for the coals to heat, and then standing in 90°F heat to make dinner while swatting mosquitoes, I can grill juicy, tender burgers in my air fryer and stay cool and calm.

Think about what you cook often in your kitchen. Grilled pork chops? Turn to the air fryer. Meat loaf? The air fryer can make it. How about Sweet and Sour Chicken (page 106)? Again, use the air fryer. Just turn it on and set the timer.

The air fryer doesn't just help you make recipes quickly. It also makes cleanup a breeze. Rinse the basket and put it in the dishwasher. Use a damp sponge to wipe down the machine, and you're done. Try to do that with a stovetop splattered with baked-on red sauce or a grill covered with hardened, burned grease.

This is my forty-fourth cookbook and my fifth air fryer book. I started my career at Pillsbury and then began writing online. I love developing recipes, creating cookbooks, and helping people get in and out of the kitchen quickly while making fabulous foods. I have slow cookers, rice cookers, indoor and outdoor grills, a deep fryer, a double oven, three microwave ovens, two toaster ovens, and a pressure cooker. But when I want to make something delicious to eat in a hurry, I turn to the air fryer. That's the difference this little appliance has made in my life.

Use this book to simplify your life. Spend less time standing over a stove and more time with your family and friends. In the process, you will feed your friends and loved ones food that is better for them, more delicious, and more satisfying.

CHAPTER 1
LIVING THE FRY LIFE

Consider the air fryer an everyday kitchen tool, not a specialized appliance. After all, you can use it to cook just about anything, so it deserves a permanent place on your countertop. In this chapter, you will learn how easy the air fryer is to use and clean. In addition to being an energy-efficient choice, the air fryer also makes food that is more delicious and healthier than other types of cooking. Learn how to make crisp fried chicken with little oil, bake fudgy brownies, grill kebabs, and perfectly roast vegetables.

Once you get comfortable using the air fryer, you will find yourself using it more and more. With the exception of a Thanksgiving turkey, the air fryer can cook just about any recipe.

An Everyday Kitchen Tool

The air fryer is an essential tool for the modern kitchen. Here are a few benefits of this appliance.

EASY TO USE

The air fryer is easy to use: Simply put food in the basket (or on a rack—more about this later), select the time and temperature, and turn it on. Other than shaking the basket or turning the food over for even cooking or crispness, the machine does all the work. Some air fryers come with preset functions and buttons for different foods, such as French fries, frozen vegetables, bacon, fish, and chicken, which eliminates any guesswork, even if you aren't following a recipe.

This appliance is energy efficient, and it won't heat up your kitchen like an oven or stovetop. An air fryer keeps heat inside the unit by using a heating coil to warm the air, then blows that hot air around with a high-speed fan.

FLAVOR BOOSTER

The air fryer acts as a flavor and texture booster. Food in an air fryer cooks quickly, allowing flavor compounds that evaporate into the air during deep-frying and sautéing to stay in the food. You'll notice that chicken tastes more chicken-y, vegetables have more flavor, and herbs and spices pack more punch.

Food gets juicier, too, with super-crunchy exteriors. Chicken, pork chops, and steak taste tender and juicy, crisp-tender vegetables retain their flavor, and baked goods have a nice crust. The air fryer's hot, fast-moving air seals the surface of food quickly, allowing it to hold in the juices. The hot air also removes water from the surface of foods, lending that coveted crunch. To create a crust, most foods get coated with flour or bread crumbs and are then sprayed with just a bit of oil. Even frozen foods, such as frozen vegetables, cook beautifully in the air fryer, going from frozen to crisp and hot in just a few minutes.

HEALTHY COOKING

The air fryer lets you make traditionally high-fat foods, such as fried chicken and French fries, with fewer calories. In fact, deep-fried recipes made in the air fryer use 90 percent less fat. The recipes in this cookbook use only a small amount of oil. When air frying, oil is poured into a mister and sprayed onto the food before it goes in the appliance.

Food cooked in an air fryer is healthy in ways you may not expect. The closed cooking environment helps to preserve nutrients. And because food cooked in an air fryer is often more flavorful with an appealing texture, your family may eat more vegetables. Who can resist a crisp yet tender broccoli floret that's flavored with herbs? You may find your child eating a browned and crisp Brussels sprout with no coaxing.

EASY CLEANUP

The air fryer is easy to clean. You simply pull out the basket, remove the food, unplug the appliance, and let the basket and air fryer cool. To keep food from sticking to it, the basket is coated with a nonstick finish (never spray the basket with nonstick cooking spray because that may damage the finish). Once the basket is cool, rinse it, add a bit of soap, rinse again, and dry. Some air fryer baskets are dishwasher safe (check the instruction manual).

If food does stick to your basket, soak the basket in soapy water for about 30 minutes, after which any food particles should come right off. Wipe the outside of the air fryer with a damp cloth. Remove any crumbs from the basket enclosure to prevent them from burning the next time you use your air fryer.

GUIDE TO FRYERS

There are many types of air fryers. The market has expanded beyond the initial stand-alone rounded fryer with a removable basket. Air fryers come in various sizes, too, allowing you to make French fries for a few people or cook an entire dinner for four.

No matter what size air fryer you have, you can make all the recipes in this book. If you have a smaller air fryer, you may need to cook the food in batches and shake the food or rearrange it once during cooking.

There are three main types of air fryers on the market:

Basket Fryer: The classic air fryer is an oval or square appliance with a large removable basket in the front next to the control buttons. Food goes in the basket, which is permeated with holes, and a fan blows heated air around the food. Some newer versions have a front window so you can see the food as it cooks.

Paddle Fryer: These air fryers have a paddle that stirs the food as it cooks, which encourages even browning and prevents food from burning. Some have bowls that move, with or without a rotating paddle. The paddle can break softer foods apart, but it's possible to remove the paddle on most models.

Oven-Style Fryer: This is the newest version on the market. This air fryer looks like a large toaster oven. A door in the front opens to allow easy access for food and pans, and a large window lets you see the food as it cooks. A metal basket hangs on hooks inside or slides into the machine to use like a basket fryer, but there are also removable wire racks. Some may have a rotisserie function for larger cuts of meat. If you bake in your air fryer, this is a good choice.

Kitchen Set-Up

You don't need to rework your kitchen to start cooking with an air fryer, but there are some tools and pantry staples that will make using your air fryer easier. These items can be found in hardware stores, kitchen supply stores, online, and in grocery stores.

TOOLS

The tools you need that make air frying more fun are inexpensive and widely available. They help you cook your food to perfection and make it easier to get food in and out of your air fryer, especially if you have a basket fryer.

Baking pans: The air fryer basket is usually 8 to 9 inches in diameter, which means you need smaller baking pans to fit in the appliance. Most baking recipes call for 6- or 7-inch round baking pans and springform pans. Smaller muffin tins and baking sheets are also useful, although you can use the bottom of a springform pan as a baking sheet. A cake barrel, a deep, round pan with a handle, is necessary for some recipes and is used often in this book, especially in main dishes. If you plan on making a lot of pizza, a pizza pan is a good addition.

Grill pan: If you plan on using the air fryer often to grill steaks or burgers, a grill pan will add those great marks to the food. The pan is slotted, so the grease will drip away from the food as it cooks.

Oil mister: Many foods need to be sprayed with a fine coat of oil before they are cooked in an air fryer, and an oil mister makes this an easy task. Coating food in oil helps it brown and prevents sticking. The oil also helps keep bread crumbs or other coatings on the food when the fan blows hot air around.

Parchment paper rounds: These come in handy when you bake a pizza or roast a chicken. The paper is precut into rounds that fit precisely in the air fryer basket. The paper is usually perforated so air can circulate around the food.

Plate lifter: This gizmo looks like a wide pair of tongs. It's essential for removing cake and pie pans from an air fryer basket. The bottom edges of the lifter grip the pans so you can get them out of the basket without using a foil sling or burning yourself.

Raised rack: A rack with legs about 2 inches tall lets you make more food in each batch. Several recipes in this book call for a raised rack; get one that's stainless steel.

Silicone-tipped, spring-loaded tongs: Tongs help you safely remove food from the air fryer and manipulate it during cooking. Many foods, such as chicken breasts and French fries, should be turned over halfway through baking to ensure the food cooks and browns evenly. Make sure that your tongs are heat-rated to 500°F.

Other silicone accessories: Silicone muffin cups, egg bite holders, brushes, and silicone mitts to fit on your fingers are all useful for working with the air fryer. Such accessories allow you to bake full-size muffins and cupcakes and, in the case of mitts, protect your hands as you remove hot food from a hot basket.

PANTRY AND REFRIGERATOR STAPLES

Certain pantry and refrigerator staples are necessary for air frying. They make cooking more interesting and help you get the best results out of your appliance.

Baking ingredients: Keep flour, granulated sugar, brown sugar, powdered sugar, baking powder, cocoa powder, baking soda, nuts, raisins, and chocolate chips on hand. Some of the bread, cake, brownie, and cookie recipes in this book use these ingredients.

Bread crumbs: Many air fryer recipes use bread crumbs to coat the food to make a crisp crust and seal in the juices. In addition to dried bread crumbs and seasoned bread crumbs, you may want to buy panko bread crumbs, which are a bit larger and sharper than regular bread crumbs and produce a shatteringly crisp crust.

Frozen and fresh meats: Chicken breasts, chicken thighs, ground beef, steaks, and pork chops all cook beautifully in the air fryer, whether they are frozen or thawed. Fresh meats also cook well in the air fryer.

Herbs and spices: A good selection of herbs and spices is essential to any type of cooking. Basics include ground cinnamon, dried sage, dried thyme, dried oregano, chili powder, ground ginger, ground cumin, garlic powder, onion powder, and cayenne pepper. Some of the recipes in this book have spice and breading mixes that you can make in quantity and keep in your pantry.

Oils with high smoke points: Most foods cooked in the air fryer need to be coated with a small amount of oil to brown evenly. Oil is used in stir-fry recipes and also to spray on food before it's cooked. Oil also ensures that bread crumbs used for coating will stick to the food. (See Know Your Oils, page 7, for more on smoke points.)

Produce: Frozen veggies are great for the air fryer, but fresh veggies also work in this appliance. Keep potatoes, onions, and garlic in the pantry, but most fresh produce should be refrigerated.

KNOW YOUR OILS

Oils are important in air fryer cooking. They are used in batters and to coat the food so it browns and crisps evenly. These recipes only use a bit of oil, but the type of oil you choose is crucial. Some oils are better than others when it comes to air frying because of their smoke point, or the temperature at which the oil breaks down and smokes. Choose an oil with a smoke point above 400°F, or your food won't taste good.

Avocado oil: With a smoke point of 520°F, this oil is the most stable of the bunch. It is flavorless, high in monounsaturated fats, and low in saturated fats.

Olive oil: Regular olive oil, not extra-virgin, is the oil of choice for the air fryer. It has a smoke point of 460°F and is light in flavor and color.

Peanut oil: This oil has a smoke point of 450°F. It is light and essentially flavorless, making it perfect to use on all types of foods.

Safflower oil: This oil has a smoke point of 510°F. It is light and flavorless and is high in polyunsaturated fats.

Soybean oil: The smoke point of this oil is 470°F. It is flavorless and high in polyunsaturated fats.

Air Fryer Basics

Even if you've used an air fryer before, it's a good idea to read this section for a quick refresher on how to best use this appliance. There are some things you should know to get the best results from your air fryer.

SET-UP

When you get your air fryer home, the first thing to do is unpack it. Remove all packing material and put the air fryer on your counter. Then, read the instruction manual cover to cover. That manual offers tips and tricks on using the appliance, as well as safety warnings, information about the warranty, and troubleshooting tips. It may also include recipes.

Your air fryer should be placed on a stable and heatproof surface, at least five inches between the back of the fryer and the wall, and with at least five inches of space above it. Make sure an electrical outlet is nearby; do not use an extension cord. The air fryer can produce a lot of heat, so you may want to put a silicone pad under it if you have Formica or granite countertops.

Keep kids and pets away from the air fryer. The appliance itself can get hot, and the vent in the back or on top of the air fryer will blow hot air.

After you read the manual, familiarize yourself with the buttons and programs, how the basket fits in the air fryer, and any accessories that may have been packed in the box.

COOKING

Many recipes require preheating your air fryer. Set the cooking temperature and let it heat to temperature. Some air fryers do not require preheating: Check your instruction manual.

Food cooked in an air fryer basket will cook and brown more evenly if it is cut into pieces of similar size and shape. Otherwise, you may have undercooked or burnt pieces of food.

Fill the basket according to the recipe. If you preheated the air fryer, be careful—the basket will be hot. Most foods can be stacked to cook, as long as you don't overfill the basket and you shake or turn the food halfway through the cooking time. Some foods need to be placed in a single layer. If you have an oven-type air fryer, you can put food on the racks or use the basket.

Once the food is in the basket, insert the basket so it sits securely in the base. Set the timer—choose the shorter time period so the food doesn't overcook—and let the machine work. You can pull out the basket to check on progress at any time: The air fryer will turn off and then turn back on automatically when the basket is reinserted.

Only use ovenproof accessories that are marketed for air fryer use. Be careful when adding pans to the air fryer basket; a plate lifter or a foil sling will help.

CLEANUP AND TROUBLESHOOTING

Cleaning your air fryer is a breeze. First, remove the food and put the basket back in the air fryer. If you have an oven-type air fryer, put either the basket or racks back in. Turn the air fryer off, unplug it, and let it cool.

Once the appliance is cool, remove the basket and/or racks and clean them with warm, soapy water. If any food is stuck to the basket or racks, soak the basket and/or racks in warm soapy water until the food loosens. Some baskets or racks are dishwasher-safe; check your instruction manual. Finally, wipe out the inside of the air fryer with a damp cloth (make sure it's unplugged!), clean the outside, and relax.

The main complaint about cooking with an air fryer is that it hasn't properly crisped the food. That's often because the food was too wet when it started cooking. To avoid limp food, pat wet foods dry, coat some foods in flour or bread crumbs, and spray the food with oil before cooking.

If white smoke comes out from the air fryer vent, it could mean that the food was too wet. Some of that "smoke" may be steam. Black smoke, however, is a sign that something is wrong. If you see black smoke, turn off the machine, unplug it, let it cool, and get it to a repair shop.

Another common issue with new air fryers is a plastic smell. This should go away after a few uses. You can let the machine "outgas" by taking it out of the box and putting it in the garage or on the porch for a couple of days. Another fix is to put an equal amount of lemon juice and apple cider vinegar in a small ovenproof bowl. Put the bowl in the basket and run the air fryer at 400°F for about 5 minutes. Let it stand for 15 minutes and then remove the bowl. Once the air fryer is cool, wipe the inside with a damp cloth. Clean the basket, and you should be ready to go.

7 SECRETS TO
PERFECT FRYING, EVERY TIME

These tips will help you achieve the perfect golden-brown crisp with your air fryer, every time.

1. Do not overload the basket. The recipe will tell you how to arrange the food in the air fryer basket. Some foods such as French fries and other veggies can be stacked, while others should be placed in a single layer in the basket.

2. Should you preheat? It depends on your air fryer. Read that instruction booklet again. Some air fryers recommend preheating for 2 to 3 minutes, while others can cook without preheating.

3. Shake the basket or turn food over halfway through the cooking time to help it cook and brown evenly. When you shake or turn the food, you may want to spray it again with your oil mister for even browning.

4. Check for doneness at the earliest time in the recipe. Vegetables are done when they are hot and tender and crisp. Cakes, cookies, and brownies are done when they are set to the touch. Meats are done when they are cooked to a safe final internal temperature. You should use a food thermometer to make sure beef and pork cuts are cooked to 145°F; poultry, including ground chicken and turkey, to 165°F; seafood to 145°F; and ground beef and egg dishes to 160°F.

5. Do not use too much oil. An oil mister puts the perfect amount of oil on foods. Too much oil will drip off the food and may burn and create smoke.

6. Do not use a liquid batter to coat food. It will drip off the food, burn, and cause a mess. Most air-fried foods are coated with bread crumbs, ground nuts, or cheese.

7. Adapt your old favorite conventional recipes to the air fryer. To make an oven recipe in your air fryer, simply lower the cooking temperature by 25°F and reduce the cooking time by 20 to 30 percent.

Get Creative

Now that your air fryer is unpacked, you've read the instruction manual, you understand how the air fryer works, you've collected a few accessories, and you know the tips and tricks for best results, it's time to start having fun. Let's experiment with different foods and flavor profiles.

After making a few of this book's recipes, use the charts on pages 160–167, which specify cooking times for your favorite frozen and fresh ingredients, to do your own creative mixing and experimenting. Be sure to follow the basic rules of air frying: Don't overcrowd the basket, do spritz food with oil, and do check for doneness at the earliest time. If you experiment, write down the ingredient list and cooking time so you can reproduce your masterpiece.

One of the best ways to vary a recipe is to change the flavor profile by choosing a different meat, veggie, or fruit. If you find a recipe for roasted apples with cinnamon bread crumbs, for instance, substitute pears for apples and change the breading to crushed crisp cereal with cardamom. A recipe for chicken with sweet potatoes could be changed to turkey with carrots. Have fun.

Another way to vary a recipe is by using different herbs and spices. Some of these recipes have spice mixes and breading mixtures you can vary according to your tastes. For instance, if you love the flavors of Indian food, you can substitute curry powder or curry paste for dried oregano and garlic powder. If you are a fan of Italian food, use dried oregano, basil, and thyme in place of other herbs. Start by experimenting with small amounts of your own spice mixes to make sure you like the taste. Then, you can prepare enough to fill a small spice bottle to have on hand whenever you want to get creative.

About the Recipes

The recipes in this book cover the basic foods that everyone makes in the air fryer, such as French fries and chicken wings, but you'll also find some surprising new takes, such as Shrimp Fried Rice (page 76), Bagel Pizzas (page 123), and Lemon Bars (page 154). Some of these recipes require accessories, but you won't need anything more complicated than a cake pan, muffin cups, or a pizza pan.

When you make these recipes, remember that cooking times depend on your fryer make and size. That means you start with the cooking times in this book, then add a little more time as needed until the food is crisp and perfectly done. Check the food early, because you can always add more cooking time, but it's impossible to fix burned or overcooked food.

These recipes were chosen for ease of preparation, good taste, and interesting variations on classics. We've thrown in a few foods inspired by cultures from around the globe that you'll want to add to your repertoire, too. The recipes highlight the versatility of the air fryer to bake, grill, fry, roast, and stir-fry.

All the recipes are labeled with defining words to help you choose the right ones for you. Recipes labeled Family Favorite feed at least four people and use kid-friendly ingredients. Those filed under 30-Minute can be prepared and cooked in 30 minutes. Gluten-Free indicates a recipe made without wheat for celiac patients and anyone who avoids gluten. Vegetarian or Vegan means the recipe is meat-free or it excludes all animal products.

Pick a recipe or three, and let's start cooking! You'll find lots of new favorite foods in this book and have lots of fun, too.

Crunchy Nut Granola, page 26

CHAPTER 2
BREAKFAST

Flaky Maple Donuts

30-MINUTE, FAMILY FAVORITE

MAKES
15 DONUTS
_____

PREP TIME
10 minutes
_____

COOK TIME
15 minutes, plus
1 hour to cool
_____

PREHEAT
325°F
_____

PER SERVING
(1 DONUT)
Calories: 109
Total fat: 3g
Saturated fat: 1g
Cholesterol: 4mg
Sodium: 32mg
Carbohydrates: 21g
Fiber: 0g
Protein: 0g

This donut is made from puff pastry, so it bakes into a flaky, tender square that you dip in a fragrant maple glaze. Find puff pastry in the grocery store's freezer section. These square donuts don't waste dough or require a special donut cutter.

1 frozen puff pastry sheet (15 by 10 inches), thawed

2 teaspoons all-purpose flour

2½ cups powdered sugar

3 tablespoons pure maple syrup

2 tablespoons 2% milk

2 tablespoons butter, melted

½ teaspoon vanilla extract

½ teaspoon ground cinnamon

Pinch salt

1. Put the puff pastry on a work surface dusted with the flour. Cut into 15 squares by cutting crosswise into five 3-inch-wide strips and then cutting each strip into thirds.

2. Set or preheat the air fryer to 325°F. Put a parchment paper round in the bottom of the basket and add as many pastry squares as will fit without touching or overlapping.

3. Bake for 14 to 19 minutes or until the donuts are browned and not doughy inside. Cool on a wire rack. Repeat with the remaining dough.

4. In a small bowl, combine the powdered sugar, maple syrup, milk, melted butter, vanilla, cinnamon, and salt and mix with a wire whisk until combined.

5. Let the donuts cool for about 1 hour, then dip the top half of each in the glaze. Turn the donut over, glaze-side up, and put on wire racks. Let stand until set, then serve.

FRY FACT Use a food thermometer to check the internal temperature of a donut. It should be 210°F.

INGREDIENT TIP Maple syrup is graded according to color and flavor: Golden, Amber, Dark, and Very Dark. They all taste good; the only difference is that as the syrup gets darker, the flavor gets more intense. Buy the least expensive type you can as long as it is labeled "pure maple syrup."

Coffeecake Muffins

FAMILY FAVORITE

MAKES
6 MUFFINS

PREP TIME
20 minutes

COOK TIME
15 minutes, plus
10 minutes to cool

PREHEAT
330°F

PER SERVING
(1 MUFFIN)
Calories: 285
Total fat: 11g
Saturated fat: 7g
Cholesterol: 57mg
Sodium: 122mg
Carbohydrates: 42g
Fiber: 1g
Protein: 4g

Muffins made in the air fryer? This super quick recipe is perfect for weekday mornings. The streusel filling and topping make these muffins an irresistible treat.

1⅓ cups all-purpose flour, divided

5 tablespoons butter, melted, divided

¼ cup packed light brown sugar

½ teaspoon ground cinnamon

⅓ cup granulated sugar

¼ cup 2% milk

1 large egg

1 teaspoon vanilla extract

1 teaspoon baking powder

Pinch salt

Nonstick baking spray (containing flour)

1. In a small bowl, combine ⅓ cup of flour, 2½ tablespoons of butter, the brown sugar, and cinnamon and mix until crumbly. Set the streusel topping aside.

2. In a medium bowl, combine the remaining 2½ tablespoons of butter, the granulated sugar, milk, egg, and vanilla and mix well.

3. Add the remaining 1 cup flour, baking powder, and salt and mix just until combined.

4. Spray 6 silicone muffin cups with baking spray.

5. Spoon half of the batter into the prepared muffin cups. Top each with about 1 teaspoon of the streusel, then add the remaining batter. Sprinkle each muffin with the remaining streusel and gently press into the batter.

6. Set or preheat the air fryer to 330°F. Place the muffin cups in the air fryer basket. Bake the muffins for 14 to 18 minutes or until a toothpick inserted into the center of a muffin comes out clean. Cool on a wire rack for 10 minutes, then remove the muffins from the silicone cups. Serve warm or cold.

MAKE IT A MEAL Serve these muffins with Eggs in Purgatory (page 24) or Veggie Frittata (page 28) for a satisfying breakfast. Pair with orange juice and coffee, of course.

Baked Oatmeal Apple Cups

FAMILY FAVORITE, GLUTEN-FREE

SERVES 6

PREP TIME
15 minutes

COOK TIME
15 minutes, plus
15 minutes to cool

PREHEAT
350°F

PER SERVING
(1 APPLE CUP)
Calories: 254
Total fat: 8g
Saturated fat: 3g
Cholesterol: 43mg
Sodium: 82mg
Carbohydrates: 40g
Fiber: 4g
Protein: 8g

These little cups might taste like an oatmeal cookie, but they make a great breakfast, thanks to tasty, wholesome ingredients, including oatmeal, egg, applesauce, chopped apple, and cinnamon. Double this recipe so you have enough for another breakfast or two.

½ cup unsweetened applesauce

1 large egg

⅓ cup packed light brown sugar

2 tablespoons butter, melted

½ cup 2% milk

1⅓ cups old-fashioned rolled oats

1 teaspoon ground cinnamon

½ teaspoon baking powder

Pinch salt

½ cup diced peeled apple

Nonstick baking spray (containing flour)

1. In a medium bowl, combine the applesauce, egg, brown sugar, melted butter, and milk and mix until combined.

2. Add the oats, cinnamon, baking powder, and salt and stir until mixed. Stir in the apple.

3. Spray 6 silicone muffin cups with baking spray. Divide the batter among the muffin cups.

4. Set or preheat the air fryer to 350°F. Place the muffin cups in the air fryer basket. Bake the cups for 13 to 18 minutes or until they are set to the touch. Let cool for 15 minutes before serving.

INGREDIENT TIP If you're avoiding gluten, be sure the oats you buy are gluten-free. Some oats are processed in the same facility as wheat, so read the label. Gluten-free oatmeal will be labeled as such.

Bacon-Roasted Fruit *with* Yogurt

FAMILY FAVORITE, GLUTEN-FREE

SERVES 4

PREP TIME
15 minutes

COOK TIME
20 minutes

PREHEAT
350°F and 380°F

PER SERVING
Calories: 211
Total fat: 7g
Saturated fat: 4g
Cholesterol: 24mg
Sodium: 203mg
Carbohydrates: 30g
Fiber: 3g
Protein: 8g

When you roast fruit, it becomes tender and sweet with complex flavors. The air fryer is the perfect appliance for roasting fruit. The fruit in this recipe is roasted in a bit of bacon fat for even more flavor. Serve it over Greek yogurt.

3 bacon slices

1 Granny Smith apple, peeled and cubed

1 Bosc pear, peeled and cubed

1 cup canned cubed pineapple

2 tablespoons sugar

½ teaspoon ground cinnamon

2 cups plain Greek yogurt

1. Put a rack inside a 7-inch cake pan. Cut the bacon slices in half crosswise and put them on the rack.

2. Set or preheat the air fryer to 350°F. Place the cake pan in the air fryer basket. Cook the bacon for 7 minutes, then check for doneness. Cook for another 2 to 3 minutes, if necessary, until crisp.

3. Remove the bacon from the rack and place on paper towels to drain. Remove the rack and scoop all but 2 teaspoons of bacon fat out of the pan.

4. Set or preheat the air fryer to 380°F. Add the apple, pear, and pineapple to the fat in the pan. Sprinkle with the sugar and cinnamon and toss.

5. Roast the fruit for 10 to 15 minutes, stirring the mixture every 5 minutes, until the fruit is tender and browned around the edges.

6. Crumble the bacon and add it to the fruit; serve over the yogurt.

LOVING YOUR LEFTOVERS Do not discard the excess bacon fat. You can use it as a base for many different soups, especially bean soups. It's also great for making crisp roasted potatoes, cooked in the air fryer, of course.

INGREDIENT TIP You can make this a vegetarian recipe by omitting the bacon. Instead, toss the fruit with 2 teaspoons safflower or sunflower oil and sprinkle with the sugar and cinnamon. Continue with the recipe.

Scrambled Eggs *with* Cheese

SERVES 4

PREP TIME
5 minutes

COOK TIME
14 minutes

PREHEAT
350°F

PER SERVING
Calories: 371
Total fat: 31g
Saturated fat: 16g
Cholesterol: 433mg
Sodium: 551mg
Carbohydrates: 2g
Fiber: 0g
Protein: 20g

Scrambled eggs make a delicious and quick breakfast, and this recipe adds shredded cheese for more flavor and protein. Use any type of cheese you'd like.

8 large eggs

¼ cup sour cream

¼ cup whole milk

¼ teaspoon salt

Pinch freshly ground black pepper

3 tablespoons butter, divided

1 cup shredded Cheddar cheese

1 tablespoon minced fresh chives

1. In a medium bowl, beat the eggs with the sour cream, milk, salt, and pepper until foamy.

2. Put 2 tablespoons of butter in a cake barrel, put it in the air fryer, and set or preheat to 350°F. The butter will melt while the air fryer preheats.

3. Remove the barrel from the air fryer basket. Add the egg mixture to the cake barrel and return to the air fryer.

4. Cook for 4 minutes, then stir the eggs with a heatproof spatula.

5. Cook for 3 minutes more minutes, then stir again.

6. Cook for 3 minutes more minutes, then add the remaining 1 tablespoon of butter and the Cheddar and stir gently.

7. Cook for 2 to 4 more minutes or until the eggs are just set.

8. Remove the cake barrel from the air fryer and put the eggs in a serving bowl. Sprinkle with the chives and serve.

LOVING YOUR LEFTOVERS If you have leftover scrambled eggs, use them to make an egg quesadilla. Cover the eggs and refrigerate. When you're ready, sprinkle a flour tortilla with some grated cheese and top with bits of the scrambled egg mixture. Add more cheese and fold the tortilla in half. Air fry at 325°F for 5 to 6 minutes, flipping halfway through the cooking time, until the tortilla is crisp and the cheese melted.

Soda Bread Currant Muffins

FAMILY FAVORITE

SERVES 6

———

PREP TIME
15 minutes

———

COOK TIME
15 minutes, plus
10 minutes to cool

———

PREHEAT
350°F

———

PER SERVING
Calories: 204
Total fat: 7g
Saturated fat: 4g
Cholesterol: 47mg
Sodium: 140mg
Carbohydrates: 32g
Fiber: 2g
Protein: 5g

Soda bread is a traditional Irish recipe that is usually served on St. Patrick's Day. Currants add chewiness and sweetness. Serve these muffins warm with some room-temperature butter.

1 cup all-purpose flour

2 tablespoons whole wheat flour

1 teaspoon baking powder

⅛ teaspoon baking soda

Pinch salt

3 tablespoons light brown sugar

½ cup dried currants

1 large egg

⅓ cup buttermilk

3 tablespoons butter, melted

Nonstick baking spray (containing flour)

1. In a medium bowl, combine the flours, baking powder, baking soda, salt, and brown sugar and mix until combined. Stir in the currants.

2. In a small bowl, combine the egg, buttermilk, and melted butter and stir until blended.

3. Add the egg mixture to the flour mixture and stir just until combined.

4. Spray 6 silicone muffin cups with baking spray. Divide the batter among the muffin cups, filling each about two-thirds full.

5. Set or preheat the air fryer 350°F. Set the muffin cups in the air fryer basket. Bake the muffins for 14 to 18 minutes or until a toothpick inserted in the center comes out clean.

6. Cool on a wire rack for 10 minutes before serving.

INGREDIENT TIP Dried currants are smaller than raisins, so they are better in these smaller muffins. They are in the baking aisle of the grocery store right next to the raisins. If you can't find them, substitute dark or golden raisins.

Raspberry-Stuffed French Toast

30-MINUTE, FAMILY FAVORITE

SERVES 4

PREP TIME
15 minutes

COOK TIME
8 minutes

PREHEAT
375°F

PER SERVING
Calories: 278
Total fat: 6g
Saturated fat: 3g
Cholesterol: 99mg
Sodium: 406mg
Carbohydrates: 46g
Fiber: 2g
Protein: 9g

French toast is the perfect recipe for the air fryer. The bread is stuffed with fresh raspberries and raspberry jam, soaked in egg and milk, and air-fried to crisp perfection.

4 (1-inch-thick) slices French bread

2 tablespoons raspberry jam

⅓ cup fresh raspberries

2 egg yolks

⅓ cup 2% milk

1 tablespoon sugar

½ teaspoon vanilla extract

3 tablespoons sour cream

1. Cut a pocket into the side of each bread slice, making sure you don't cut through to the other side.

2. In a small bowl, combine the raspberry jam and raspberries and crush the raspberries into the jam with a fork.

3. In a shallow bowl, beat the egg yolks with the milk, sugar, and vanilla until combined.

4. Spread some of the sour cream in the pocket you cut in the bread slices, then add the raspberry mixture. Squeeze the edges of the bread slightly to close the opening.

5. Dip the bread in the egg mixture, letting the bread stand in the egg for 3 minutes. Flip the bread over and let stand on the other side for 3 minutes.

6. Set or preheat the air fryer to 375°F. Arrange the stuffed bread in the air fryer basket in a single layer.

7. Air fry for 5 minutes, then carefully flip the bread slices and cook for another 3 to 6 minutes, until the French toast is golden brown.

LOVING YOUR LEFTOVERS The leftover egg whites can be used in several ways. Freeze them and use in recipes, or you can use them to coat meats or fish before breading and air frying them. Or make an egg white omelet.

FRY FACT This method of cooking French toast is lower in fat than frying the bread in butter.

Apple Roll-Ups

FAMILY FAVORITE

MAKES
8 ROLL-UPS

PREP TIME
20 minutes

COOK TIME
20 minutes

PREHEAT
350°F

PER SERVING
(2 ROLL-UPS)
Calories: 232
Total fat: 15g
Saturated fat: 9g
Cholesterol: 38mg
Sodium: 249mg
Carbohydrates: 21g
Fiber: 4g
Protein: 4g

In this recipe, the apples are cooked, then rolled in bread, dipped in butter and a homemade spice mix, and air-fried until hot and crisp.

3 tablespoons ground cinnamon

3 tablespoons granulated sugar

2 teaspoons ground nutmeg

1 teaspoon ground cardamom

½ teaspoon ground allspice

2 large Granny Smith apples, peeled and cored

10 tablespoons butter, melted, divided

2 tablespoons light brown sugar

8 thin slices white sandwich bread, crusts cut off

1. For the spice mix: In a small bowl, combine the cinnamon, granulated sugar, nutmeg, cardamom, and allspice and mix well. Transfer the spice mix to a small screw-top glass jar. (Some of the mix is used in this recipe; save the rest for other uses.)

2. Cut the apples into ½-inch pieces. Place the pieces in a cake barrel or cake pan and drizzle with 2 tablespoons of melted butter. Sprinkle with the brown sugar and 1 teaspoon of the spice mix and toss.

3. Set or preheat the air fryer to 350°F. Set the pan in the air fryer basket. Cook the apples for 8 to 12 minutes or until they are tender but still hold their shape. Remove the pan from the air fryer and put the apples in a bowl to cool.

4. Roll each slice of sandwich bread with a rolling pin until it is about ¼ inch thick.

5. Top each slice of bread with 2 tablespoons of the apple mixture, then roll it up. Dip the roll-ups in the remaining 8 tablespoons of melted butter and sprinkle each with about ½ teaspoon of spice mix.

6. Put the rolls, seam-side down, in a pan lined with a round of parchment paper, and air fry for 6 to 9 minutes or until the bread is browned and crisp. Serve warm.

MAKE IT A MEAL These are delicious served with Scrambled Eggs with Cheese (page 20). Or, serve them with Veggie Frittata (page 28).

Eggs *in* Purgatory

GLUTEN-FREE, VEGETARIAN

SERVES 4

PREP TIME
15 minutes

COOK TIME
30 minutes, plus
10 minutes to cool

PREHEAT
375°F

PER SERVING
Calories: 132
Total fat: 8g
Saturated fat: 2g
Cholesterol: 186mg
Sodium: 370mg
Carbohydrates: 7g
Fiber: 2g
Protein: 7g

Eggs in Purgatory is the colorful name for eggs cooked in a slightly spicy tomato sauce. The typical recipe uses whole eggs that are cooked soft set, but this recipe scrambles the eggs into the sauce. Serve with whole wheat toast for a satisfying breakfast.

1 tablespoon olive oil

2 cups cherry tomatoes, halved

½ cup chopped plum tomatoes

¼ cup tomato sauce

2 scallions, sliced

2 garlic cloves, minced

1 teaspoon honey

½ teaspoon salt

⅛ teaspoon cayenne pepper

4 large eggs

1. In a 7-inch springform pan that has been wrapped in foil to prevent leaks, combine the olive oil, cherry tomatoes, plum tomatoes, tomato sauce, scallions, garlic, honey, salt, and cayenne.

2. Set or preheat the air fryer to 375°F. Set the pan in the air fryer basket. Cook the tomato mixture for 15 to 20 minutes, stirring twice during the cooking time, until the tomatoes are soft.

3. Use a fork to mash some of the tomatoes right in the pan, then stir the mashed tomatoes into the sauce.

4. Break the eggs into the sauce. Return the pan to the air fryer.

5. Cook for about 2 minutes or until the egg whites start to set. Remove the pan from the air fryer and gently stir the eggs into the sauce, marbling them through the sauce. Don't mix them in completely.

6. Continue cooking the mixture until the eggs are just set, 4 to 8 minutes more.

7. Cool for 10 minutes, then serve.

INGREDIENT TIP Cherry tomatoes are a good choice for this recipe because their quality is high year-round. When beefsteak tomatoes are in season, use those instead. You'll need about 2 cups chopped, seeded tomatoes, no matter what kind you choose.

Pepper Egg Bites

30-MINUTE, FAMILY FAVORITE, GLUTEN-FREE, VEGETARIAN

MAKES
7 EGG BITES

PREP TIME
15 minutes

COOK TIME
15 minutes, plus
5 minutes to cool

PREHEAT
325°F

PER SERVING
(1 EGG BITE)
Calories: 87
Total fat: 6g
Saturated fat: 3g
Cholesterol: 141mg
Sodium: 149mg
Carbohydrates: 1g
Fiber: 0g
Protein: 7g

Made popular by coffee shop chains, egg bites are mini crustless quiches made in a silicone egg bite pan that you can buy online. Each pan has seven indentations that you fill with an egg mixture and cook until firm in the air fryer.

5 large eggs, beaten

3 tablespoons 2% milk

½ teaspoon dried marjoram

⅛ teaspoon salt

Pinch freshly ground black pepper

⅓ cup minced bell pepper, any color

3 tablespoons minced scallions

½ cup shredded Colby or Muenster cheese

1. In a medium bowl, combine the eggs, milk, marjoram, salt, and black pepper; mix until combined.

2. Stir in the bell peppers, scallions, and cheese.

3. Fill the 7 egg bite cups with the egg mixture, making sure you get some of the solids in each cup.

4. Set or preheat the air fryer to 325°F. Make a foil sling: Fold an 18-inch-long piece of heavy-duty aluminum foil lengthwise into thirds. Put the egg bite pan on this sling and lower it into the air fryer. Leave the foil in the air fryer, but bend down the edges so they fit in the appliance.

5. Bake the egg bites for 10 to 15 minutes or until a toothpick inserted into the center comes out clean.

6. Use the foil sling to remove the egg bite pan. Let cool for 5 minutes, then invert the pan onto a plate to remove the egg bites. Serve warm.

FRY FACT More fragile recipes such as this one, along with cakes and quiches, may need to be covered with foil about halfway through the cooking time so the top doesn't brown too much. Check the food about halfway through cooking time. If it's getting too brown, add foil.

Crunchy Nut Granola

30-MINUTE, FAMILY FAVORITE

SERVES 6

PREP TIME
10 minutes

COOK TIME
15 minutes

PREHEAT
325°F

PER SERVING
Calories: 446
Total fat: 18g
Saturated fat: 5g
Cholesterol: 15mg
Sodium: 51mg
Carbohydrates: 64g
Fiber: 7g
Protein: 11g

Homemade granola is easy to make and tastes much better than granola from a box. Once you try it, you'll never buy the packaged stuff again. You can customize this recipe using your favorite nuts and dried fruit. Double this recipe and have some on hand all week.

2 cups old-fashioned rolled oats

¼ cup pistachios

¼ cup chopped pecans

¼ cup chopped cashews

¼ cup honey

2 tablespoons light brown sugar

3 tablespoons butter

½ teaspoon ground cinnamon

Nonstick baking spray (containing flour)

½ cup dried cherries

1. In a medium bowl, combine the oats, pistachios, pecans, and cashews and toss.

2. In a small saucepan, combine the honey, brown sugar, butter, and cinnamon. Cook over low heat, stirring frequently, until the butter melts and the mixture is smooth, about 4 minutes. Pour over the oat mixture and stir.

3. Spray a 7-inch springform pan with baking spray. Add the granola mixture.

4. Set or preheat the air fryer to 325°F. Set the pan in the air fryer basket. Cook for 7 minutes, then remove the pan and stir. Continue cooking for 6 to 9 minutes or until the granola is light golden brown. Stir in the dried cherries.

5. Remove the pan from the air fryer and let cool, stirring a couple of times as the granola cools. Store in a covered container at room temperature up to 4 days.

MAKE IT A MEAL   Serve this granola on top of a scoop of Greek yogurt for a satisfying breakfast. Add orange juice and some fresh fruit on the side.

Breakfast Pizzas

30-MINUTE, FAMILY FAVORITE

Pizza doesn't have to be made on a traditional crust. This recipe uses toasted French bread cut on a diagonal so there's more surface area for toppings—in this case, scrambled eggs, bacon, and cheese.

4 (½-inch-thick) slices French bread, cut on a diagonal

6 teaspoons butter, divided

4 large eggs

2 tablespoons light cream

½ teaspoon dried basil

¼ teaspoon sea salt

⅛ teaspoon freshly ground black pepper

4 bacon slices, cooked until crisp and crumbled

⅔ cup shredded Colby or Muenster cheese

1. Spread each slice of bread with 1 teaspoon of butter and place in the air fryer basket.

2. Set or preheat the air fryer to 350°F. Toast the bread for 2 to 3 minutes or until it's light golden brown. Remove from the air fryer and set aside on a wire rack.

3. Melt the remaining 2 teaspoons of butter in a 6-inch cake pan in the air fryer for 1 minute. Remove the basket from the air fryer.

4. In a medium bowl, beat together the eggs, cream, basil, salt, and pepper and add to the melted butter in the pan. Return the basket to the air fryer. Cook for 3 minutes, then stir. Cook for another 3 to 5 minutes or until the eggs are just set. Remove the eggs from the pan and put them in a bowl.

5. Top the bread with the scrambled eggs mixture, bacon, and cheese. Put back in the air fryer basket. Cook for 4 to 8 minutes or until the cheese is melted and starting to turn brown in spots.

6. Let cool for 5 minutes and serve.

SPICE IT UP You can make these pizzas mild or spicy. Use pepper Jack cheese or add minced jalapeños to the scrambled eggs. Or, sprinkle them with red pepper flakes before baking.

Veggie Frittata

FAMILY FAVORITE, GLUTEN-FREE, VEGETARIAN

SERVES 4

PREP TIME
15 minutes

COOK TIME
25 minutes

PER SERVING
Calories: 260
Total fat: 21g
Saturated fat: 11g
Cholesterol: 277mg
Sodium: 463mg
Carbohydrates: 2g
Fiber: 0g
Protein: 15g

A frittata is a cross between a quiche and an omelet, kind of like a crustless quiche. It's easy to make, and you can vary it any way you'd like. Serve this frittata hot out of the pan, after it's cooled for 20 minutes, or even cold right from the refrigerator.

¼ cup chopped red bell pepper

¼ cup chopped yellow summer squash

2 tablespoons chopped scallion

2 tablespoons butter

5 large eggs, beaten

¼ teaspoon sea salt

⅛ teaspoon freshly ground black pepper

1 cup shredded Cheddar cheese, divided

1. In a 7-inch cake pan, combine the bell pepper, summer squash, and scallion. Add the butter.

2. Set or preheat the air fryer to 350°F. Set the cake pan in the air fryer basket. Cook the vegetables for 3 to 4 minutes or until they are crisp-tender. Remove the pan from the air fryer.

3. In a medium bowl, beat the eggs with the salt and pepper. Stir in half of the Cheddar. Pour into the pan with the vegetables.

4. Return the pan to the air fryer and cook for 10 to 15 minutes, then top the frittata with the remaining cheese. Cook for another 4 to 5 minutes or until the cheese is melted and the frittata is set. Cut into wedges to serve.

SUBSTITUTION TIP Use any soft or cooked vegetable in this frittata. You can use peas, zucchini, chopped seeded tomatoes, or even leftover hash brown potatoes. Just cook them until they are crisp but tender, as in step 2.

Spicy Hash Brown Potatoes

FAMILY FAVORITE, GLUTEN-FREE, VEGAN

SERVES 4

PREP TIME
15 minutes, plus
10 minutes to soak

COOK TIME
20 minutes

PREHEAT
400°F

PER SERVING
Calories: 235
Total fat: 8g
Saturated fat: 1g
Cholesterol: 0mg
Sodium: 419mg
Carbohydrates: 39g
Fiber: 5g
Protein: 5g

The best potatoes to use for hash browns are russets because they are high in starch and low in moisture. They crisp to golden brown, while staying tender inside.

2 tablespoons chili powder

2 teaspoons ground cumin

2 teaspoons smoked paprika

1 teaspoon garlic powder

1 teaspoon cayenne pepper

1 teaspoon freshly ground black pepper

2 large russet potatoes, peeled

2 tablespoons olive oil

⅓ cup chopped onion

3 garlic cloves, minced

½ teaspoon sea salt

1. For the spice mix: In a small bowl, combine the chili powder, cumin, smoked paprika, garlic powder, cayenne, and black pepper. Transfer to a screw-top glass jar and store in a cool, dry place. (Some of the spice mix is used in this recipe; save the rest for other uses.)

2. Grate the potatoes in a food processor or on the large holes of a box grater. Put the potatoes in a bowl filled with ice water, and let stand for 10 minutes.

3. When the potatoes have soaked, drain them, then dry them well with a kitchen towel.

4. Put the olive oil, onion, and garlic in a 7-inch cake pan.

5. Set or preheat the air fryer to 400°F. Put the onion mixture in the air fryer and cook for 3 minutes, then remove.

6. Put the grated potatoes in a medium bowl and sprinkle with 2 teaspoons of spice mixture and toss. Add to the cake pan with the onion mixture.

7. Cook in the air fryer for 10 minutes, then stir the potatoes gently but thoroughly. Cook for 8 to 12 minutes more or until the potatoes are crisp and light golden brown. Season with salt.

Sage *and* Pear Sausage Patties

FAMILY FAVORITE, GLUTEN-FREE

SERVES 6

PREP TIME
15 minutes

COOK TIME
20 minutes

PREHEAT
375°F

PER SERVING
Calories: 204
Total fat: 16g
Saturated fat: 6g
Cholesterol: 54mg
Sodium: 236mg
Carbohydrates: 1g
Fiber: 0g
Protein: 13g

The slight bitterness of the sage contrasts with the mild sweetness of the pork and pear in these breakfast sausages. These patties work as well for weekend brunch as they do for a quick weekday breakfast. To save time, double this recipe, form the patties, and then freeze half for later use.

1 pound ground pork

¼ cup diced fresh pear

1 tablespoon minced fresh sage leaves

1 garlic clove, minced

½ teaspoon sea salt

⅛ teaspoon freshly ground black pepper

1. In a medium bowl, combine the pork, pear, sage, garlic, salt, and pepper, and mix gently but thoroughly with your hands.

2. Form the mixture into 8 equal patties about ½ inch thick.

3. Set or preheat the air fryer to 375°F. Arrange the patties in the air fryer basket in a single layer. You may have to cook the patties in batches.

4. Cook the sausages for 15 to 20 minutes, flipping them halfway through the cooking time, until a meat thermometer registers 160°F. Remove from the air fryer, drain on paper towels for a few minutes, and then serve.

MAKE IT A MEAL Serve these flavorful little sausage patties with Scrambled Eggs with Cheese (page 20) or Spicy Hash Brown Potatoes (page 30) and some fresh fruit.

Tex-Mex Cheese Sticks, page 41

CHAPTER 3
SNACKS AND APPETIZERS

Guacamole Bombs

FAMILY FAVORITE, GLUTEN-FREE, VEGETARIAN

SERVES 6

PREP TIME
15 minutes, plus
3 hours to freeze

COOK TIME
10 minutes

PREHEAT
400°F

PER SERVING
(2 GUACAMOLE
BOMBS)
Calories: 205
Total fat: 17g
Saturated fat: 3g
Cholesterol: 31mg
Sodium: 209mg
Carbohydrates: 11g
Fiber: 7g
Protein: 6g

Everyone loves guacamole. But have you ever had fried guacamole? This unusual and delicious recipe is easy to make. You just have to plan ahead because these guac bombs have to freeze for 3 hours or they fall apart when fried. Serve this at a party and watch them disappear.

2 avocados

1 tablespoon minced fresh parsley

1 tablespoon fresh lemon juice

½ teaspoon salt

1 egg, beaten

1 tablespoon 2% milk

¼ cup almond flour

½ cup finely ground almonds

Olive oil, for misting

1. Peel and pit the avocados, remove the flesh, and mash in a medium bowl along with the parsley, lemon juice, and salt.

2. Line a baking sheet with parchment paper. Form the avocado mixture into 12 balls using a small ice cream scoop or an ⅛-cup measure, and place them on the lined baking sheet. Freeze until firm, about 3 hours.

3. In a shallow bowl, beat the egg with the milk. Combine the almond flour and ground almonds on a plate.

4. Dip the frozen guacamole in the egg mixture, then roll in the almond mixture to coat.

5. Set or preheat the air fryer to 400°F. Place 6 of the bombs in the air fryer basket and mist with olive oil. Put the other 6 bombs back in the freezer while you cook the first batch.

6. Cook for 4 to 5 minutes or until the bombs are light golden brown. Repeat with the second batch, then serve.

SPICE IT UP Serving the guacamole with very few seasonings allows the flavor of the avocado to come through, but you could add minced jalapeños, chopped scallion, red pepper flakes, or chili powder to the avocado mixture before you freeze it.

Brie *and* Bacon Mini Tartlets

30-MINUTE, FAMILY FAVORITE

SERVES 6

———

PREP TIME
10 minutes

———

COOK TIME
18 minutes

———

PREHEAT
400°F and 350°F

———

PER SERVING
Calories: 198
Total fat: 9g
Saturated fat: 4g
Cholesterol: 23mg
Sodium: 395mg
Carbohydrates: 19g
Fiber: 1g
Protein: 8g

The combination of bacon and melted cheese is always a favorite. Put them together in crisp little tartlet shells for a fabulous appetizer you can serve at parties. You can cook the bacon and cube the cheese ahead of time and assemble these little tartlets just before you want to cook them.

6 bacon slices

16 frozen mini phyllo tartlet shells

½ cup diced Brie cheese

3 tablespoons apple jelly

1. Set or preheat the air fryer to 400°F. Carefully place the bacon in a single layer in the air fryer basket. Cook for 7 minutes, then carefully turn each piece of bacon and cook for 6 to 7 minutes more.

2. Remove the bacon from the basket and drain on paper towels. Crumble when cool and set aside. Pour the bacon fat out of the air fryer basket. Let the basket cool for 10 minutes, then wipe it out with a paper towel.

3. Fill the tartlet shells with the bacon and the Brie cubes. Put a bit of apple jelly on top of the filling in each shell.

4. Set or preheat the air fryer to 350°F. Put the filled shells in the air fryer basket. Cook for 5 to 6 minutes or until the cheese is melted and the tartlet shells are light brown. Remove and serve.

INGREDIENT TIP It's easier to dice Brie cheese if you freeze it for 1 hour first. Cut off the rind and then dice the interior.

Curly Fries

SERVES 4

PREP TIME
15 minutes, plus
30 minutes to soak

COOK TIME
12 minutes

PREHEAT
400°F

PER SERVING
Calories: 176
Total fat: 4g
Saturated fat: 0g
Cholesterol: 0mg
Sodium: 300mg
Carbohydrates: 33g
Fiber: 2g
Protein: 4g

Curly fries are a fun twist on traditional French fries. You do need a spiralizer to make these potatoes, although it's possible to pierce a potato with a skewer and rotate a knife around the potato to cut one big spiral. Serve with ketchup or dipping sauce of your choice.

2 large russet potatoes, peeled

1 tablespoon olive oil

½ teaspoon sea salt

¼ teaspoon freshly ground black pepper

1. Put the potatoes through the spiralizer, cutting them into 4- to 5-inch lengths. Place the potatoes in a large bowl, cover with cold water, and let stand for 30 minutes.

2. Drain the potatoes and pat dry in a kitchen towel. In a bowl, drizzle the potatoes with the olive oil and season with the salt and pepper; toss well.

3. Set or preheat the air fryer to 400°F. Add half of the potatoes to the air fryer basket and cook for 5 minutes. Toss the potatoes in the basket and cook for another 5 to 7 minutes or until the potatoes are golden brown and crisp.

4. Repeat with the remaining potatoes.

5. You can put all the potatoes back in the basket and cook for another 1 to 2 minutes so they are all hot when you serve them.

SPICE IT UP Sprinkle the finished curly fries with just about any herb or spice. Or, use 1 to 2 teaspoons of the spice mix from Spicy Hash Brown Potatoes (page 30) or Spanish-Inspired Chicken Wings (page 48).

FRY FACT For crispier, fast food–style fries, dredge the spiralized potatoes in equal parts flour and cornstarch before cooking.

Everything Bagel Snack Mix

30-MINUTE, FAMILY FAVORITE, VEGETARIAN

SERVES 6

PREP TIME
10 minutes

COOK TIME
8 minutes, plus
1 hour to cool

PREHEAT
325°F

PER SERVING
Calories: 507
Total fat: 31g
Saturated fat: 9g
Cholesterol: 21mg
Sodium: 873mg
Carbohydrates: 50g
Fiber: 4g
Protein: 12g

Everything bagel seasoning is so versatile. You can use it on any-thing from toast to chicken, but it's especially good in this crisp and crunchy snack mix that uses bagel chip crumbs. Serve this snack on game day or as an after-school snack.

1 cup bagel chips, crushed

¼ cup poppy seeds

¼ cup sesame seeds

2 tablespoons dried minced onion

1 tablespoon dried minced garlic

1 teaspoon salt

2 cups Rice Chex cereal

2 cups small square cheese crackers

1 cup small pretzels

1 cup unsalted cashews

4 tablespoons (½ stick) butter, melted

1. For the everything bagel breading mix: In a small bowl, combine the bagel chip crumbs, poppy seeds, sesame seeds, dried onion, dried garlic, and salt. Transfer the breading mix to a small screw-top glass jar. (Some of the breading mix is used in this recipe; save the rest for other uses. Store at room temperature for up to 3 weeks.)

2. In a medium bowl, combine the Rice Chex cereal, cheese crack-ers, pretzels, and cashews. Drizzle with the melted butter and toss to coat.

3. Set or preheat the air fryer to 325°F. Put the snack mixture in the air fryer basket. Cook for 4 minutes. Shake the basket, then cook for another 3 to 5 minutes or until the snack mix is glazed and has turned slightly darker brown.

4. Remove from the air fryer and immediately toss the snack mixture with 2 tablespoons of the everything bagel breading mix. Let cool for about 1 hour before serving.

SUBSTITUTION TIP Just about any small snack food can be used in this recipe. Try mixed nuts, cheese puffs, Bugles, cheese crackers of any shape, bagel chips, and other types of cereal.

Fried Ravioli *with* Spicy Dipping Sauce

30-MINUTE, FAMILY FAVORITE, VEGETARIAN

SERVES 6

PREP TIME
10 minutes

COOK TIME
12 minutes

PREHEAT
350°F

PER SERVING
Calories: 400
Total fat: 26g
Saturated fat: 6g
Cholesterol: 65mg
Sodium: 510mg
Carbohydrates: 30g
Fiber: 2g
Protein: 11g

Fried stuffed pasta is an appetizer with universal appeal. These little ravioli are coated in bread crumbs and ground almonds for lots of crunch, then air-fried until crisp. A simple spicy dipping sauce completes the dish beautifully.

10-ounce bag frozen mini round ravioli

1 egg

2 tablespoons light cream

½ cup dried bread crumbs

¼ cup ground almonds

2 tablespoons grated Parmesan cheese

Cooking oil, for misting

⅔ cup mayonnaise

2 tablespoons Dijon mustard

2 garlic cloves, minced

¼ teaspoon red pepper flakes

1. Keep the ravioli frozen until you're ready to cook. In a shallow bowl, beat the egg with the cream. Put the bread crumbs, almonds, and Parmesan on a plate and mix.

2. Dip the ravioli in the egg mixture, then toss in the bread crumb mixture to coat.

3. Set or preheat the air fryer to 350°F. Put half of the ravioli in the air fryer basket and mist with cooking oil. Cook for 10 to 12 minutes, shaking once during the cooking time, until the ravioli are hot and crisp and browned on the outside. Repeat with the remaining ravioli.

4. Meanwhile, in a small bowl, combine the mayonnaise, mustard, garlic, and pepper flakes and mix well.

5. Serve the ravioli with the sauce.

LOVING YOUR LEFTOVERS If you have leftover ravioli, cover and refrigerate them overnight. The next day, heat them in the air fryer for a couple of minutes, then toss them into a green salad for a great lunch.

Mini Blooming Onions

FAMILY FAVORITE, VEGETARIAN

SERVES 4

PREP TIME
20 minutes

COOK TIME
15 minutes, plus
10 minutes to cool

PREHEAT
375°F

PER SERVING
Calories: 262
Total fat: 3g
Saturated fat: 1g
Cholesterol: 94mg
Sodium: 648mg
Carbohydrates: 50g
Fiber: 4g
Protein: 9g

Blooming onions are a fun, interactive appetizer. Traditionally, the dish is served as a large battered, deep-fried onion that's been cut so everyone can pull off wedges to eat. This air fryer recipe uses smaller onions for individual servings, and delivers crisp, browned onions. Serve with guacamole or salsa for a winning appetizer.

4 to 6 small (2-inch) onions (see Tip)

1 cup all-purpose flour

1 teaspoon salt

½ teaspoon paprika

1 teaspoon cayenne pepper

2 eggs

2 tablespoons 2% milk

Cooking oil, for misting

1. To prepare the onions, carefully peel them. Then, cut ½ inch off the stem ends and trim the root ends.

2. Place the onions root-side down on a cutting surface. Cut the onions into quarters, making sure not to cut all the way through the bottoms. Cut each quarter into two sections. Gently pull the wedges apart, being careful not to break them.

3. Put the flour, salt, paprika, and cayenne in a shallow bowl. In a separate shallow bowl, beat the eggs with the milk.

4. Dip the onions in the flour, getting the flour into the onion as much as possible. Dip in the egg mixture, coating thoroughly, then in the flour mixture again. Shake off excess flour.

5. Set or preheat the air fryer to 375°F. Arrange the onions cut-side up in the air fryer basket, and mist them with cooking oil. Cook for 10 to 15 minutes or until the onions are golden brown and crisp but tender on the inside. Let cool for 10 minutes, then serve.

INGREDIENT TIP Buy more onions than you need, so if you break one or two you can still make the full recipe. The broken onions can be chopped up and stored in the fridge to be used in another recipe in the next day or two.

FRY FACT This recipe is much healthier than a typical deep-fried blooming onion.

Tex-Mex Cheese Sticks

30-MINUTE, FAMILY FAVORITE, VEGETARIAN

SERVES 4

PREP TIME

10 minutes, plus
1 hour to freeze

COOK TIME

10 minutes

PREHEAT

375°F

PER SERVING

Calories: 299
Total fat: 19g
Saturated fat: 9g
Cholesterol: 91mg
Sodium: 531mg
Carbohydrates: 14g
Fiber: 2g
Protein: 19g

Cheese sticks are the quintessential appetizer, and the air fryer is the best way to cook them. These string cheese treats are usually either deep-fried, which adds fat, or baked, which doesn't properly crisp the coating. You need to plan ahead, because the sticks must be frozen after they are coated in the crumb mixture.

1 egg, beaten

½ cup dried bread crumbs

¼ cup ground peanuts

1 tablespoon chili powder

¼ teaspoon red pepper flakes

⅛ teaspoon cayenne pepper

8 mozzarella string cheese sticks

Cooking oil, for misting

1. Place the beaten egg in a shallow bowl. Combine the bread crumbs, peanuts, chili powder, pepper flakes, and cayenne on a plate.

2. Dip each piece of string cheese in the egg and then in the bread crumb mixture. Put the sticks on a baking sheet lined with parchment paper and freeze for 30 minutes.

3. Repeat the breading routine. Freeze the sticks for another 30 minutes.

4. Set or preheat the air fryer to 375°F. Place 4 sticks in the air fryer basket in a single layer (don't let them touch), and mist them with cooking oil. (Return the remaining sticks to the freezer.) Cook for 7 to 9 minutes or until the outsides are golden brown and the insides are hot and melted.

5. Repeat with the remaining sticks. Serve hot with marinara or ranch sauce for dipping.

FRY FACT This is a great recipe to prepare in advance and store in your freezer. When you use the air fryer, you can have hot and melty cheese sticks in less than 10 minutes.

Cheesy Bacon Cranberry Dip

30-MINUTE, FAMILY FAVORITE

SERVES 6

———

PREP TIME
15 minutes

———

COOK TIME
15 minutes

———

PREHEAT
350°F

———

PER SERVING
Calories: 248
Total fat: 21g
Saturated fat: 10g
Cholesterol: 55mg
Sodium: 393mg
Carbohydrates: 7g
Fiber: 0g
Protein: 9g

This warm, cheesy dip has the most wonderful combination of textures and flavors. Crisp, salty bacon is combined with melty Brie cheese and tart and tangy dried cranberries. For dipping, use breadsticks, toasted French bread slices, and fresh apple slices.

4 ounces cream cheese, at room temperature

3 tablespoons mayonnaise

1 cup diced Brie cheese

½ teaspoon dried thyme

4 bacon slices, cooked until crisp and crumbled

⅓ cup dried cranberries

1. In a medium bowl, beat the cream cheese with the mayonnaise until blended. Stir in the Brie, thyme, bacon, and cranberries. Put the dip mixture in a 6-inch round pan.

2. Set or preheat the air fryer to 350°F. Set the pan in the air fryer basket. Cook for 5 minutes, then remove and stir. Continue cooking for another 5 to 7 minutes or until the dip is melted and bubbling.

SUBSTITUTION TIP Consider adding other ingredients to the base of cream cheese, mayonnaise, and Brie to make different dips. Try adding cooked and drained sausage, replace the bacon with cooked small shrimp, or replace the cranberries with chopped bell peppers or artichoke hearts.

Shrimp Cashew Egg Rolls

30-MINUTE, FAMILY FAVORITE

SERVES 6

PREP TIME
20 minutes

COOK TIME
12 minutes

PREHEAT
350°F and 400°F

PER SERVING
Calories: 369
Total fat: 10g
Saturated fat: 2g
Cholesterol: 101mg
Sodium: 843mg
Carbohydrates: 50g
Fiber: 3g
Protein: 19g

Egg rolls are perfect for the air fryer. These little bundles turn out tender and hot on the inside and crisp on the outside. They can be filled with anything you'd like, but this recipe uses tender shrimp, cashews, carrots, corn, and scallions.

2 tablespoons olive oil

1 onion, chopped

2 garlic cloves, minced

½ cup shredded carrots

1 pound cooked medium shrimp, peeled and chopped

1 cup frozen corn kernels, thawed

⅓ cup coarsely chopped salted cashews

1 tablespoon reduced-sodium soy sauce

2 teaspoons oyster sauce

12 egg roll wrappers

Cooking oil, for misting

1. In a 6-inch metal pan, combine the olive oil, onion, garlic, and carrots.

2. Set or preheat the air fryer to 350°F. Set the pan in the air fryer basket. Cook the vegetables for 3 to 5 minutes, stirring once, until crisp-tender. Remove the pan from the air fryer and put the vegetables in a medium bowl.

3. Add the shrimp, corn, cashews, soy sauce, and oyster sauce to the vegetables and stir to combine.

4. Put the egg roll wrappers on the work surface and brush the edges with a bit of water. Divide the filing among them. Brush the edges with water. Roll up, folding in the sides, completely enclosing the filling.

5. Set or preheat the air fryer to 400°F. Place 3 or 4 of the egg rolls in the air fryer basket and mist with cooking oil. Cook for 6 minutes, turn, mist with more oil, and cook for 3 to 5 minutes more or until the egg rolls are browned and crisp. Repeat with remaining egg rolls. Serve hot.

SPICE IT UP You can make these egg rolls spicy by adding a minced jalapeño pepper or two, and ⅛ teaspoon cayenne pepper to the filling. Or add 1 to 2 teaspoons of the spice mix from Mexican Street Corn (page 64).

Parsnip Chips

30-MINUTE, GLUTEN-FREE, VEGAN

SERVES 6

PREP TIME
15 minutes

COOK TIME
15 minutes

PREHEAT
400°F

PER SERVING
Calories: 109
Total fat: 5g
Saturated fat: 0g
Cholesterol: 0mg
Sodium: 397mg
Carbohydrates: 16g
Fiber: 5g
Protein: 1g

Parsnips are root vegetables that look like large white carrots. They are not as sweet as carrots, though, and are often treated more like potatoes. In fact, when they are sliced thinly and cooked crisp into chips, parsnips become a crave-worthy snack.

2 large parsnips, peeled

2 tablespoons garlic oil

1 teaspoon salt

1 teaspoon smoked paprika

1. Cut the parsnips into thin (about ⅛-inch-thick) slices using a mandoline or a sharp knife. You can also use a vegetable peeler.

2. In a medium bowl, drizzle the parsnip slices with the garlic oil. Sprinkle with the salt and smoked paprika and toss to coat.

3. Put about half of the chips in the air fryer basket. Cook for 12 to 16 minutes, shaking the basket halfway through cooking time, until the chips start to turn light golden brown and aren't quite crisp. They will crisp as they cool. Spread the chips on paper towels to cool.

4. Repeat with the remaining parsnip chips. Store in an airtight container at room temperature for 3 to 4 days.

SPICE IT UP   To turn these chips into Sour Cream and Onion Parsnip Chips, mix 2 tablespoons buttermilk powder, 2 teaspoons onion powder, ½ teaspoon garlic powder, and 2 teaspoons minced dried chives in a small bowl. Omit the smoked paprika. When the chips are done, toss with the buttermilk powder mixture and cool.

FRY FACT   These unusual chips are a great substitute for potato chips. They are healthier, too, because you don't deep-fry them.

Individual Spinach Dip Bread Bowls

30-MINUTE, FAMILY FAVORITE

SERVES 8

PREP TIME
15 minutes

COOK TIME
15 minutes

PREHEAT
350°F

PER SERVING
Calories: 404
Total fat: 26g
Saturated fat: 11g
Cholesterol: 50mg
Sodium: 892mg
Carbohydrates: 29g
Fiber: 1g
Protein: 13g

What if you could have that warm, creamy, and cheesy spinach dip that's so popular in restaurants at home? These little appetizers—spinach dip baked in individual bread bowls—are perfect for a party and also make a great afternoon snack.

1 (16.3-ounce) can refrigerated biscuit dough

4 ounces cream cheese, at room temperature

¼ cup mayonnaise

1 cup frozen cut-leaf spinach, thawed and squeezed dry (see Tip)

2 bacon slices, cooked until crisp and crumbled

2 scallions, chopped

1½ cups shredded Havarti cheese, divided

½ cup shredded Muenster cheese

½ teaspoon garlic powder

1. Divide the biscuit dough into 8 biscuits. Press each one into and up the sides of a silicone muffin cup; set aside.

2. In a medium bowl, combine the cream cheese and mayonnaise and beat until smooth. Stir in the spinach, bacon, scallions, 1 cup of Havarti, the Muenster, and garlic powder.

3. Divide the cream cheese mixture among the biscuits in the muffin cups.

4. Set or preheat the air fryer to 350°F. Put 4 muffin cups in the air fryer basket. Top each with 1 tablespoon of the remaining Havarti cheese. Cook for 8 to 13 minutes or until the biscuit dough is brown and the filling is hot and bubbling. Remove from the air fryer and cool on a wire rack.

5. Repeat with the remaining filled biscuits. Serve warm.

INGREDIENT TIP Make sure you buy cut-leaf spinach and not a block of frozen spinach, because you will be unable to separate the block. To thaw, put the spinach in a colander and run it under warm water. To drain, squeeze the spinach, then wrap it in paper towels and squeeze some more before you add the spinach to the recipe.

Crisp Bacon Polenta Rounds

FAMILY FAVORITE, GLUTEN-FREE

SERVES 6

PREP TIME
10 minutes

COOK TIME
30 minutes, plus
15 minutes to cool

PREHEAT
400°F

PER SERVING
Calories: 311
Total fat: 21g
Saturated fat: 6g
Cholesterol: 32mg
Sodium: 552mg
Carbohydrates: 25g
Fiber: 1g
Protein: 6g

Polenta is cooked cornmeal. You can find it in most grocery stores in round tubes, which makes this recipe a snap. The polenta is sliced into rounds and air-fried until crisp, then topped with bacon and mixed with a lot of creamy ingredients.

1 (18-ounce) tube precooked polenta

1 tablespoon garlic oil

4 ounces cream cheese, at room temperature

3 tablespoons mayonnaise

2 scallions, sliced

1 tablespoon minced fresh chives

6 bacon slices, cooked until crisp and crumbled

1. Set or preheat the air fryer to 400°F.

2. Slice the polenta crosswise into 12 rounds. Carefully brush both sides of the rounds with the garlic oil and put 6 rounds in the air fryer basket. Set a rack in the basket over the polenta and add the remaining 6 polenta rounds.

3. Cook the polenta for 15 minutes, then flip each round and cook for another 10 to 15 minutes or until the polenta is crisp and light golden brown.

4. Meanwhile, in a small bowl, beat the cream cheese and mayonnaise until smooth. Stir in the scallions, chives, and bacon.

5. When the polenta is done, remove to a wire rack and cool for 15 minutes. Top with the bacon mixture and serve.

INGREDIENT TIP If you can't find precooked polenta in a tube, you can make your own. In a saucepan, combine 1½ cups polenta with 4½ cups vegetable or chicken stock. Cook, stirring frequently, until thick, about 10 minutes. Pour into a greased 8-inch square pan and refrigerate overnight. The next day, cut the polenta into 12 rectangles and proceed with the recipe.

Pierogi *with* Sour Cream *and* Veggie Dip

30-MINUTE, FAMILY FAVORITE, VEGETARIAN

SERVES 6

PREP TIME
10 minutes

COOK TIME
10 minutes

PREHEAT
400°F

PER SERVING
Calories: 206
Total fat: 10g
Saturated fat: 5g
Cholesterol: 26mg
Sodium: 374mg
Carbohydrates: 25g
Fiber: 2g
Protein: 5g

Fabulous as an appetizer, pierogi are large half-moons of stuffed pasta, usually filled with potatoes, cheese, and onion. Serve them with a sour cream dip that includes chopped fresh veggies for a contrasting crunch. Make the dip ahead of time, and store it covered in the refrigerator.

1 cup sour cream

1 tablespoon fresh lemon juice

½ cup chopped red bell pepper

3 scallions, chopped

½ cup shredded carrot

1 teaspoon dried thyme

1 (16-ounce) package frozen pierogi

Cooking oil, for misting

1. In a medium bowl, stir together the sour cream and lemon juice. Add the bell pepper, scallions, carrot, and thyme and mix well. Set the dip aside.

2. Set or preheat the air fryer to 400°F. Place as many frozen pierogi as will fit in a single layer in the air fryer basket and mist with cooking oil. Cook for 8 minutes.

3. Carefully, using tongs, turn each pierogi over, mist with more oil, and cook for 3 to 5 minutes more or until golden brown.

4. Repeat with the remaining pierogi. Serve hot with the dip.

SPICE IT UP   The dip is smooth and creamy and mild in this recipe. For a spicier version, add a minced jalapeño or minced chipotle in adobo. You could also sprinkle the pierogi with cayenne pepper or red pepper flakes when they come out of the air fryer.

Spanish-Inspired Chicken Wings

FAMILY FAVORITE

SERVES 4

PREP TIME
20 minutes

COOK TIME
25 minutes

PREHEAT
380°F

PER SERVING
Calories: 368
Total fat: 16g
Saturated fat: 4g
Cholesterol: 128mg
Sodium: 423mg
Carbohydrates: 4g
Fiber: 1g
Protein: 53g

There's a reason that chicken wings are a favorite game-day appetizer. They are crunchy, savory, tender, and so fun to eat. This recipe uses chicken drumettes, the meatiest part of the wing. The Spanish breading mix that coats the wings can be used in many other recipes.

1 cup finely crushed cracker crumbs

1 tablespoon sweet paprika

1 tablespoon smoked paprika

1 tablespoon cayenne pepper

1 teaspoon sea salt

2 teaspoons onion powder

1 teaspoon garlic powder

2 pounds chicken drumettes

2 tablespoons olive oil

1. To make the breading mix: In a small bowl, combine the cracker crumbs, sweet paprika, smoked paprika, cayenne, sea salt, onion powder, and garlic powder and mix well. Transfer to a screw-top glass jar. (Some of the breading mix is used in this recipe; save the rest for other uses. Store at room temperature.)

2. Put the drumettes in a large bowl, drizzle with the olive oil, and toss to coat. Sprinkle ⅓ cup of the breading mix over the meat and press the mixture onto the drumettes.

3. Set or preheat the air fryer to 380°F. Put the coated drumettes in the air fryer basket (cook in two batches if you have a smaller air fryer). Cook for 10 minutes, then shake the basket and use tongs to turn the drumettes.

4. Cook for another 12 to 16 minutes, shaking the basket halfway through cooking time, until the wings register 165°F on an instant-read thermometer and are golden brown and crisp.

INGREDIENT TIP Chicken wings have three parts to them: the tip, the flat, and the drumette. The drumette is the meatiest part and looks like the drumstick, but smaller (thus the name drumette). If you can't find drumettes in the store, you can buy whole chicken wings and cut them apart at the joints. Discard the tips (or save them for stock), and save the flats for stock or other recipes.

Crisp Beet Fries *with* Guacamole

SERVES 4

PREP TIME
20 minutes

COOK TIME
20 minutes

PREHEAT
375°F

PER SERVING
Calories: 345
Total fat: 19g
Saturated fat: 4g
Cholesterol: 93mg
Sodium: 732mg
Carbohydrates: 36g
Fiber: 11g
Protein: 11g

Fries made out of beets are incredible. Their beautiful color contrasts nicely with the bright green guacamole in this recipe. They taste sweet and tender and get a wonderful crunch from the panko. Make these beet fries for a special dinner or an everyday snack.

2 avocados, cubed

2 tablespoons fresh lemon juice

1 teaspoon sea salt, divided

2 large beets, peeled

2 eggs, beaten

1 cup panko bread crumbs

½ teaspoon paprika

Cooking oil, for misting

1. In a bowl, mash together the avocados, lemon juice, and ½ teaspoon of salt. Transfer the guacamole to a serving bowl, cover, and refrigerate.

2. Cut the beets into sticks that are 3 inches long and ½ inch thick. Put the beaten eggs in a shallow bowl, and combine the panko and paprika on a plate.

3. Dip the fries in the egg, then in the panko mixture, pressing to coat.

4. Set or preheat the air fryer to 375°F. Arrange half of the beets in the air fryer basket and mist with cooking oil. Cook for 18 to 22 minutes or until crisp and golden.

5. Repeat with remaining beets. Serve with the guacamole.

INGREDIENT TIP   Always wear disposable plastic gloves when you work with beets, or your fingers will be colored pink for days. When the beets are cooked, the color transfer is lessened.

Twice-Baked Potatoes, page 56

CHAPTER 4
VEGETABLES

Crispy Mushrooms

30-MINUTE, FAMILY FAVORITE, VEGETARIAN

SERVES 4

PREP TIME
10 minutes

COOK TIME
16 minutes

PREHEAT
400°F

PER SERVING
Calories: 94
Total fat: 2g
Saturated fat: 0g
Cholesterol: 33mg
Sodium: 296mg
Carbohydrates: 15g
Fiber: 1g
Protein: 5g

Crispy mushrooms are a snap to make in the air fryer. The mushrooms are coated in flour, egg, and bread crumbs, then fried until crunchy outside and juicy inside. They are delicious served alongside a grilled steak or roasted chicken. Or, they can be part of a vegetarian feast.

1 (8-ounce) package
cremini mushrooms

⅓ cup all-purpose flour

1 egg, beaten

⅔ cup panko bread crumbs

½ teaspoon smoked paprika

½ teaspoon salt

⅛ teaspoon freshly ground
black pepper

Cooking oil, for misting

1. Rinse the mushrooms, removing any dirt, and pat dry. Cut the mushrooms through the stems into quarters.

2. Place the flour on a plate and the egg in a shallow bowl. On a separate plate, combine the panko, smoked paprika, salt, and pepper and mix well.

3. Dip the mushrooms in the flour, then in the egg, and finally in the panko mixture, pressing to coat. Place the coated mushrooms on a wire rack as you work.

4. Set or preheat the air fryer to 400°F. Add as many mushrooms to the air fryer basket as will fit in a single layer. Mist lightly with cooking oil. Cook the mushrooms for 6 to 8 minutes, flipping them over halfway through, until they are crisp.

5. Repeat with remaining mushrooms.

FRY FACT These mushrooms are lower in calories and fat than the deep-fried mushrooms you would get at a restaurant.

Hasselback Fingerling Potatoes

FAMILY FAVORITE, GLUTEN-FREE, VEGETARIAN

SERVES 4

PREP TIME
20 minutes

COOK TIME
25 minutes

PREHEAT
400°F

PER SERVING
Calories: 142
Total fat: 6g
Saturated fat: 3g
Cholesterol: 7mg
Sodium: 610mg
Carbohydrates: 19g
Fiber: 3g
Protein: 3g

A Hasselback potato is sliced crosswise into rounds that stay connected along the base of the potato. As they cook, the potato slices fan out, the skin gets crisp, and the inside becomes tender. These little fingerling potatoes are a great variation on the classic larger Hasselback potato.

1 pound fingerling potatoes

1 tablespoon olive oil

1 tablespoon butter

1 teaspoon dried thyme

1 teaspoon sea salt

⅛ teaspoon freshly ground black pepper

1. Rinse the potatoes and dry. Put each potato on a work surface and put two chopsticks lengthwise on either side of each potato. This will help stop you from cutting all the way through. Make vertical, crosswise cuts in the potato, about ⅛ inch apart. Repeat with the remaining potatoes.

2. In a small microwave-safe dish, combine the olive oil and butter and microwave for 30 seconds or until melted. Stir in the thyme, salt, and pepper.

3. Put the potatoes in a large bowl and drizzle with the olive oil mixture. Toss very gently to coat.

4. Set or preheat the air fryer to 400°F. Add the potatoes to the air fryer basket. Cook for 22 to 27 minutes, carefully rearranging the potatoes halfway through the cooking time, until the potatoes are tender.

SUBSTITUTION TIP You can make larger potatoes in this fashion, too. Larger potatoes should be cooked in a single layer in the air fryer basket, and the cooking time will be longer, 30 to 40 minutes.

Twice-Baked Potatoes

FAMILY FAVORITE, GLUTEN-FREE

SERVES 4

_____

PREP TIME
15 minutes

_____

COOK TIME
1 hour, plus
10 minutes to cool

_____

PREHEAT
400°F

_____

PER SERVING
Calories: 449
Total fat: 27g
Saturated fat: 14g
Cholesterol: 64mg
Sodium: 924mg
Carbohydrates: 38g
Fiber: 3g
Protein: 16g

Twice-baked potatoes are first baked, and then their insides are scooped out and mixed with delicious ingredients, such as sour cream and crisp bacon. Finally everything is piled back inside the potato skins and baked again until hot and bubbling. Garnish with green onions or fresh herbs.

2 large russet potatoes

1 tablespoon olive oil

2 tablespoons butter

¼ cup sour cream

2 tablespoons buttermilk

4 bacon slices, cooked until crisp and crumbled

2 scallions, chopped

1 cup shredded Colby cheese

1 teaspoon sea salt

⅛ teaspoon freshly ground black pepper

¼ cup grated Parmesan cheese

1. Scrub the potatoes, rinse, and dry. Using a fork, pierce each potato several times. Rub the potatoes with the olive oil.

2. Set or preheat the air fryer to 400°F. Place the potatoes in the air fryer basket. Cook for 40 to 45 minutes or until the potatoes are tender when pierced with a fork.

3. Let the potatoes cool for 10 to 15 minutes, then cut each in half lengthwise. Cradle each potato half in a kitchen towel in your hand to protect yourself from the heat, and gingerly scoop out the flesh into a medium bowl, being careful not to cut through the potato skin.

4. Mash the potato flesh, then stir in the butter, sour cream, buttermilk, bacon, scallions, Colby cheese, salt, and pepper.

5. Pile the filling back inside the potato skins, and sprinkle with the Parmesan. Put the filled potatoes back in the air fryer basket in a single layer.

6. Cook the stuffed potatoes for another 10 to 15 minutes or until hot and starting to brown on top.

Roasted Garlic Brussels Sprouts

GLUTEN-FREE, VEGAN

SERVES 4

PREP TIME
15 minutes

COOK TIME
20 minutes

PREHEAT
375°F

PER SERVING
Calories: 84
Total fat: 4g
Saturated fat: 1g
Cholesterol: 0mg
Sodium: 320mg
Carbohydrates: 11g
Fiber: 4g
Protein: 4g

Don't let childhood memories of overcooked, soggy Brussels sprouts keep you from this recipe. Prepared in the air fryer, these garlicky sprouts will have even the haters gobbling them up. Roasting makes the sprouts tender and crisp.

1 pound Brussels sprouts

1 tablespoon olive oil

1 tablespoon fresh lemon juice

½ teaspoon sea salt

⅛ teaspoon garlic powder

4 garlic cloves, thinly sliced

1. Trim the stem ends of the Brussels sprouts and halve them lengthwise.

2. In a medium bowl, combine the olive oil, lemon juice, salt, and garlic powder; mix well. Add the halved Brussels sprouts and toss gently but thoroughly to coat.

3. Set or preheat the air fryer to 375°F. Put the Brussels sprouts in the air fryer basket. Cook for 15 to 20 minutes, shaking the basket halfway through cooking time, until the sprouts are light golden brown and crisp.

4. Sprinkle the sprouts with the garlic slices and toss. Cook for 2 to 4 minutes more or until the garlic is light golden brown.

MAKE IT A MEAL   These Brussels sprouts are delicious served with Lemony Sea Scallops (page 88) or Classic Roast Chicken (page 108). Add a green salad for the finishing touch.

Tex-Mex Crispy Broccoli

30-MINUTE, GLUTEN-FREE, VEGAN

SERVES 4

PREP TIME
10 minutes

COOK TIME
15 minutes

PREHEAT
375°F

PER SERVING
Calories: 108
Total fat: 7g
Saturated fat: 1g
Cholesterol: 0mg
Sodium: 399mg
Carbohydrates: 10g
Fiber: 4g
Protein: 4g

When broccoli is roasted, it becomes tender and sweet with crisp edges. This easy recipe is amped up with chipotle peppers in adobo sauce and chili powder.

1 pound broccoli

2 tablespoons olive oil

1 chipotle pepper in adobo sauce, minced

1 tablespoon adobo sauce (from the can)

2 teaspoons chili powder

½ teaspoon salt

⅛ teaspoon freshly ground black pepper

1. Rinse the broccoli and shake dry. Cut the broccoli into 1- to 2-inch-wide florets.

2. In a large bowl, combine the olive oil, chipotle pepper, adobo sauce, chili powder, salt, and pepper and mix well. Add the broccoli florets and toss to coat evenly.

3. Set or preheat the air fryer to 375°F. Put the broccoli in the air fryer basket. Cook for 13 to 18 minutes, shaking the basket halfway through cooking time, until the broccoli is crispy.

SUBSTITUTION TIP You can substitute cauliflower or Romanesco broccoli, which is similar to broccoli and looks like it came from a fanciful children's book, for the plain broccoli in this recipe. The cooking time remains the same.

Potatoes au Gratin

FAMILY FAVORITE, GLUTEN-FREE, VEGETARIAN

SERVES 4

———

PREP TIME

20 minutes

———

COOK TIME

30 minutes

———

PREHEAT

350°F

———

PER SERVING

Calories: 361
Total fat: 17g
Saturated fat: 11g
Cholesterol: 58mg
Sodium: 733mg
Carbohydrates: 40g
Fiber: 5g
Protein: 13g

Potatoes au gratin is a fancy way of saying potatoes cooked in a creamy, cheesy sauce. The cheese is what makes them different from scalloped potatoes. These delicious potatoes are true comfort food. Slice them with a mandoline if you have one; otherwise, a sharp knife works just fine.

4 medium Yukon Gold potatoes, peeled

Nonstick cooking spray

1 cup shredded Havarti or Muenster cheese

2 garlic cloves, minced

⅓ cup heavy (whipping) cream

⅓ cup whole milk

½ teaspoon dried marjoram

1 teaspoon sea salt

⅛ teaspoon freshly ground black pepper

2 tablespoons grated Parmesan cheese

1. Cut the potatoes into ⅛-inch-thick slices. Coat a 7-inch round pan with cooking spray. Layer the potatoes in the round pan with the cheese and garlic.

2. In a small bowl, mix together the cream, milk, marjoram, salt, and pepper. Pour slowly over the potatoes in the pan. Sprinkle with the Parmesan.

3. Set or preheat the air fryer to 350°F. Set the pan in the air fryer basket. Cook the potatoes for 25 to 35 minutes or until the potatoes are tender, the sauce is bubbling, and the top is golden brown.

MAKE IT A MEAL   This recipe is absolutely perfect served with Classic Mini Meat Loaves (page 128), Classic Roast Chicken (page 108), or Salmon en Papillote (page 78). A fruit salad is a nice accompaniment to this comfort food meal.

Dill-Roasted Carrots _and_ Parsnips

GLUTEN-FREE, VEGETARIAN

SERVES 4

PREP TIME
15 minutes

COOK TIME
25 minutes

PREHEAT
375°F

PER SERVING
Calories: 107
Total fat: 6g
Saturated fat: 4g
Cholesterol: 15mg
Sodium: 365mg
Carbohydrates: 13g
Fiber: 3g
Protein: 1g

Carrots and parsnips are delicious when cooked together with fresh dill. These are both root vegetables, but their differing color and flavor make for an interesting contrast. The veggies are sliced into rounds so they have crisp edges and tender interiors.

2 tablespoons butter

2 teaspoons honey

1 teaspoon dried dill weed

½ teaspoon sea salt

⅛ teaspoon freshly ground black pepper

2 large carrots, peeled and cut into ¼-inch-thick rounds

1 large parsnip, peeled and cut into ¼-inch thick rounds

1 tablespoon chopped fresh dill

1. In a small saucepan, combine the butter, honey, dried dill, salt, and pepper; heat over low heat until the butter melts.

2. Place the carrots and parsnip in the air fryer basket, drizzle the honey-butter mixture over the vegetables, and toss to coat.

3. Set or preheat the air fryer to 375°F. Cook the vegetables for 20 to 25 minutes or until they are tender and golden brown around the edges. Toss with the fresh dill and serve.

INGREDIENT TIP Fresh and dried herbs have different characteristics. For instance, dried dill has a smoky taste, whereas fresh dill has an anise or licorice taste. You can use both varieties in the same recipe.

Asparagus *in* Puff Pastry

FAMILY FAVORITE, VEGETARIAN

SERVES 4

PREP TIME
20 minutes

COOK TIME
15 minutes

PREHEAT
375°F

PER SERVING
Calories: 38
Total fat: 2g
Saturated fat: 1g
Cholesterol: 0mg
Sodium: 101mg
Carbohydrates: 3g
Fiber: 1g
Protein: 1g

Asparagus is already an elegant vegetable, but if you wrap it in puff pastry with a little honey mustard, you elevate it further. This recipe is fun and easy and makes the perfect side dish for a grilled steak or pork tenderloin.

8 asparagus spears

1 (10-by-15-inch) sheet frozen puff pastry, thawed

2 tablespoons honey mustard

1. Rinse the asparagus spears, and snap off the ends where they naturally break. Dry and set aside.

2. Cut the puff pastry sheet in half so you have two 10-by-7½-inch rectangles. (Return one of the rectangles to the freezer for another use.)

3. Spread the pastry with the honey mustard, then cut it into 8 strips that are 10 inches long and a little less than 1 inch wide. Wrap the pastry, honey mustard–side in, around the asparagus.

4. Set or preheat the air fryer to 375°F. Put a rack in the air fryer basket and arrange the asparagus spears on the rack. Cook for 12 to 17 minutes or until the puff pastry is golden brown.

SUBSTITUTION TIP You can make this recipe with green beans as well. Just cut the puff pastry strips in half so they are the right length to wrap around green beans.

INGREDIENT TIP Don't use frozen asparagus to make this recipe—the frozen spears are too soft and watery.

Spicy Garlic Smashed Potatoes

FAMILY FAVORITE, GLUTEN-FREE, VEGETARIAN

SERVES 4

PREP TIME
10 minutes

COOK TIME
40 minutes

PREHEAT
400°F

PER SERVING
Calories: 170
Total fat: 9g
Saturated fat: 6g
Cholesterol: 23mg
Sodium: 405mg
Carbohydrates: 21g
Fiber: 3g
Protein: 3g

Smashed potatoes are cooked until tender, then smashed with the bottom of a glass. This exposes more potato to the air fryer heat for crisp potatoes that are extra tender inside. Most recipes have you cook the potatoes in the oven or microwave, but the air fryer can do it all.

1 pound baby Yukon
Gold potatoes

½ cup vegetable broth

½ teaspoon sea salt

3 tablespoons butter

2 garlic cloves, minced

2 teaspoons chili powder

⅛ teaspoon cayenne pepper

1. Rinse the potatoes. In a 7-inch cake barrel, combine the potatoes, broth, and salt. Cover the cake barrel with foil and put it in the air fryer basket.

2. Set or preheat the air fryer to 400°F. Cook the potatoes for 20 minutes, stirring once during the cooking time, until they are almost tender.

3. Drain the potatoes and place them on a baking sheet. Using the bottom of a glass, gently smash each potato just so it cracks; you don't want to break them apart.

4. On the stovetop, in a small saucepan, combine the butter, garlic, chili powder, and cayenne; heat over low heat to melt the butter. Brush some of this mixture over the potatoes.

5. Place as many potatoes as will fit in the air fryer basket in a single layer, buttered-side down. Brush the tops with more of the butter mixture. Cook for 12 to 17 minutes, turning once, until the potatoes are crisp. You can keep the cooked potatoes warm in a 250°F oven while you air fry the remainder.

6. Repeat with remaining potatoes and the remaining butter mixture.

INGREDIENT TIP   If you're making this for children, you may want to omit the garlic, chili powder, and cayenne pepper. Instead, use dried thyme or basil.

Honey-Roasted Baby Carrots

30-MINUTE, FAMILY FAVORITE, GLUTEN-FREE, VEGETARIAN

SERVES 4

———

PREP TIME
5 minutes

———

COOK TIME
20 minutes

———

PREHEAT
375°F

———

PER SERVING
Calories: 138
Total fat: 6g
Saturated fat: 4g
Cholesterol: 15mg
Sodium: 416mg
Carbohydrates: 22g
Fiber: 3g
Protein: 1g

Baby carrots are a good choice for the air fryer. Just add seasonings and let the air fryer perform its magic. This is the perfect side dish for beef, pork, chicken, or seafood.

1 (16-ounce) bag baby carrots

2 tablespoons butter, melted

2 tablespoons honey

1 tablespoon light brown sugar

½ teaspoon sea salt

Pinch nutmeg

1. In a 6-inch metal bowl, combine the baby carrots, melted butter, honey, brown sugar, salt, and nutmeg; toss well.

2. Set or preheat the air fryer to 375°F. Place the bowl in the air fryer basket. Cook for 16 to 23 minutes, stirring once halfway through the cooking time, until the carrots are tender and glazed.

SUBSTITUTION TIP You can cook large carrots using this method, too. Use 2 to 3 large carrots, peeled and cut into ½-inch-thick rounds. The cooking time remains the same.

Mexican Street Corn

30-MINUTE, FAMILY FAVORITE, GLUTEN-FREE, VEGETARIAN

SERVES 4
_____
PREP TIME
10 minutes
_____
COOK TIME
15 minutes
_____
PREHEAT
400°F
_____
PER SERVING
Calories: 288
Total fat: 13g
Saturated fat: 4g
Cholesterol: 15mg
Sodium: 178mg
Carbohydrates: 42g
Fiber: 6g
Protein: 7g

In Mexico, street vendors often serve corn on the cob slathered with cheese and seasonings. The air fryer is one of the best ways to cook corn on the cob: The dry heat concentrates the flavors, making the kernels tender and sweet.

1 tablespoon ground coriander

1 tablespoon smoked paprika

1 teaspoon sea salt

1 teaspoon garlic powder

1 teaspoon onion powder

1 teaspoon dried lime peel

1 teaspoon cayenne pepper

4 ears corn

3 tablespoons mayonnaise

3 tablespoons grated Cotija or Parmesan cheese

1 tablespoon butter, melted

1. For the spice mix: In a small bowl, combine the coriander, paprika, salt, garlic powder, onion powder, lime peel, and cayenne pepper; mix well. Transfer to a small screw-top glass jar. (Some of the spice mix is used in this recipe; save the rest for other uses. Store at room temperature.)

2. Remove the husk and silk from the corn.

3. Set or preheat the air fryer to 400°F. Place the corn in the basket and cook for 6 to 8 minutes or until the corn is crisp-tender, rearranging the ears halfway through the cooking time.

4. Meanwhile, in a small bowl, combine the mayonnaise, cheese, and melted butter.

5. Spread the mayo mixture onto the cooked corn, return the corn to the air fryer, and cook for another 3 to 5 minutes or until the corn starts to brown in spots.

6. Remove from the air fryer and sprinkle each cob with about ½ teaspoon of the spice mix.

LOVING YOUR LEFTOVERS If you have any leftover corn, cut the kernels off the cob and refrigerate. You can stir this corn into soup or add it to casseroles. Or, add more mayo and cheese and heat it up for a great lunch along with a green salad.

Garlicky Green Beans

30-MINUTE, FAMILY FAVORITE, GLUTEN-FREE, VEGAN

SERVES 4

PREP TIME
10 minutes

COOK TIME
15 minutes

PREHEAT
375°F

PER SERVING
Calories: 88
Total fat: 4g
Saturated fat: 1g
Cholesterol: 0mg
Sodium: 302mg
Carbohydrates: 13g
Fiber: 5g
Protein: 3g

Green beans aren't always thought of as an exciting vegetable, but when cooked with garlic in the air fryer, they become irresistible. They are delicious as a side dish and can also be served as an appetizer with any dip.

1½ **pounds green beans**

1 **tablespoon olive oil**

½ **teaspoon garlic powder**

½ **teaspoon sea salt**

⅛ **teaspoon freshly ground black pepper**

4 **garlic cloves, thinly sliced**

1. Rinse the green beans and cut off a bit of both ends. In a bowl, toss the beans with the olive oil, garlic powder, sea salt, and pepper.

2. Set or preheat the air fryer to 375°F. Add the green beans to the air fryer basket. Cook for 6 minutes, shaking the basket halfway through the cooking time.

3. Add the garlic to the air fryer and shake. Cook for another 3 to 6 minutes or until the green beans are tender and the garlic slices start to brown.

SUBSTITUTION TIP   You can cook other veggies using this recipe: Try asparagus (but cut the first cook time to 3 minutes), snap or snow peas (again reducing the first cook time to 3 minutes), or wax beans.

Stir-Fried Zucchini *and* Yellow Squash

30-MINUTE, FAMILY FAVORITE, GLUTEN-FREE, VEGAN

SERVES 4

PREP TIME
15 minutes

COOK TIME
15 minutes

PREHEAT
400°F

PER SERVING
Calories: 93
Total fat: 7g
Saturated fat: 1g
Cholesterol: 0mg
Sodium: 297mg
Carbohydrates: 7g
Fiber: 2g
Protein: 2g

Zucchini and yellow squash are both at their peak in midsummer. Combine them in this easy stir-fry recipe, which adds lots of flavor to these delicate vegetables. You can make this with all zucchini or all yellow squash.

1 medium zucchini

2 medium yellow squash

3 garlic cloves, sliced

2 tablespoons olive oil

⅓ cup vegetable broth

1 tablespoon fresh lemon juice

2 teaspoons cornstarch

1 teaspoon dried basil

½ teaspoon sea salt

⅛ teaspoon freshly ground black pepper

1. Slice the zucchini and squash into ½-inch rounds. In a 7-inch metal bowl, combine the squash, garlic, and olive oil.

2. Set or preheat the air fryer to 400°F. Place the bowl in the air fryer basket. Cook the zucchini mixture for 5 minutes, stirring once during cooking time. Drain if necessary.

3. Meanwhile, in a small bowl, whisk together the broth, lemon juice, cornstarch, basil, salt, and pepper.

4. Pour the broth mixture into the metal bowl with the squash and stir. Cook for another 4 to 9 minutes, stirring twice during the cooking time, until the vegetables are tender and the sauce has thickened.

LOVING YOUR LEFTOVERS If there's any of this recipe left over, use it to make an omelet the next morning. Beat 3 eggs and cook them in a small pan on the stovetop over medium heat until almost set. Add the zucchini mixture to the eggs and sprinkle with some cheese. Fold one side of the omelet over the other, then dig in.

Mediterranean Roasted Cherry Tomatoes

30-MINUTE, FAMILY FAVORITE, GLUTEN-FREE, VEGAN

SERVES 4

PREP TIME
10 minutes

COOK TIME
10 minutes

PREHEAT
400°F

PER SERVING
Calories: 46
Total fat: 4g
Saturated fat: 0g
Cholesterol: 0mg
Sodium: 123mg
Carbohydrates: 4g
Fiber: 1g
Protein: 1g

Roasted cherry tomatoes are something special. Though this tomato variety is already nice and sweet and tender, roasting brings out even more sweetness and caramelizes parts of the tomato, so they melt in your mouth.

1 tablespoon dried oregano

1 tablespoon dried basil

2 teaspoons dried marjoram

1 teaspoon dried thyme

1 teaspoon salt

2 cups cherry tomatoes, stemmed

1 tablespoon olive oil

1. For the herb mix: In a small bowl, combine the oregano, basil, marjoram, thyme, and salt; mix well. Transfer to a small screw-top glass jar. (Some of the herb mix is used in this recipe; save the rest for other uses.)

2. Set or preheat the air fryer to 400°F. Prick each cherry tomato with a toothpick to prevent bursting.

3. Put the tomatoes and olive oil on a piece of heavy-duty aluminum foil. Sprinkle with 1½ teaspoons of the herb mix and toss. Fold the foil around the tomatoes, leaving air space in the packet, and seal loosely.

4. Put the foil packet in the air fryer. Cook for 8 to 10 minutes or until the tomatoes are tender.

SPICE IT UP   If you prefer a spicier blend, add some red pepper flakes to the herbs in the mix. Use about ¼ teaspoon, or up to 1 teaspoon if you like really spicy foods.

Honey-Roasted Acorn Squash

FAMILY FAVORITE, GLUTEN-FREE, VEGETARIAN

SERVES 4

PREP TIME
15 minutes

COOK TIME
20 minutes

PREHEAT
375°F

PER SERVING
Calories: 90
Total fat: 4g
Saturated fat: 0g
Cholesterol: 0mg
Sodium: 149mg
Carbohydrates: 16g
Fiber: 2g
Protein: 1g

Acorn squash has a sweet, golden yellow flesh. Roast this squash with honey and cardamom for a delicious side dish that you might serve with a pot roast in winter. If you can't find cardamom, substitute nutmeg.

1 acorn squash

1 tablespoon honey

1 tablespoon safflower oil

¼ teaspoon cardamom

¼ teaspoon sea salt

1. Cut the acorn squash in half lengthwise and remove the seeds. Cut each half crosswise into 1-inch-wide half-circles, then cut each half-circle in half again to make quarter rounds.

2. In a medium bowl, combine the honey, oil, cardamom, and salt; mix well. Add the squash and toss with the honey mixture to coat.

3. Set or preheat the air fryer to 375°F. Add the coated squash to the air fryer basket. Cook for 15 to 20 minutes, shaking the basket halfway through cooking time, until the squash is tender and starting to brown around the edges.

SUBSTITUTION TIP You can cook other varieties of winter squash using this method. Try butternut squash, pie pumpkins, delicata squash, or kabocha squash. Each has a slightly different flavor.

Apples 'n' Onions

30-MINUTE, FAMILY FAVORITE, GLUTEN-FREE, VEGETARIAN

SERVES 4

PREP TIME
15 minutes

COOK TIME
15 minutes

PREHEAT
325°F

PER SERVING
Calories: 142
Total fat: 5g
Saturated fat: 2g
Cholesterol: 8mg
Sodium: 317mg
Carbohydrates: 24g
Fiber: 3g
Protein: 1g

Apples and onions are an old-fashioned combination that is really delicious. Remember that onions taste sweet when they are roasted, so the flavor blends well with the apples. Give it a try the next time you're serving roast pork for dinner.

1 large onion, sliced

2 teaspoons safflower oil

2 Granny Smith or McIntosh apples, peeled and sliced

2 tablespoons light brown sugar

1 tablespoon honey

1 tablespoon butter, melted

½ teaspoon sea salt

1. In a 6-inch metal bowl, toss the onion slices with the oil to coat.

2. Set or preheat the air fryer to 325°F. Place the bowl in the air fryer basket. Cook the onions for 5 minutes.

3. Remove the bowl from the air fryer basket. Add the apples, brown sugar, honey, melted butter, and sea salt and stir. Remember that the bowl is hot.

4. Return the bowl to the air fryer basket and cook for 10 to 12 minutes or until the onions and apples are tender. Stir again and serve.

SPICE IT UP For a sweet-and-spicy twist on this recipe, add ⅛ teaspoon cayenne pepper and a minced chipotle pepper in adobo.

Stir-Fried Cabbage *in* Honey Mustard

GLUTEN-FREE, VEGETARIAN

SERVES 4

PREP TIME
15 minutes

COOK TIME
20 minutes

PREHEAT
375°F

PER SERVING
Calories: 192
Total fat: 15g
Saturated fat: 2g
Cholesterol: 6mg
Sodium: 119mg
Carbohydrates: 14g
Fiber: 3g
Protein: 2g

If you love cabbage, you probably love mustard, too. This spicy and fragrant side dish combines the best of both. When cabbage is cooked, it becomes tender and silky and slightly sweet. The mustard provides the perfect spicy contrast.

4 cups chopped green cabbage

1 small onion, chopped

2 garlic cloves, minced

2 tablespoons olive oil

⅓ cup creamy honey mustard salad dressing

1 tablespoon fresh lemon juice

1 tablespoon cornstarch

½ teaspoon celery seeds

1. In a 7-inch cake barrel, toss together the cabbage, onion, and garlic. Add the olive oil and toss.

2. Set or preheat the air fryer to 375°F. Cook the cabbage mixture for 10 minutes or until the cabbage is slightly wilted. Drain off any excess liquid.

3. While the cabbage is cooking, in a small bowl, combine the salad dressing, lemon juice, cornstarch, and celery seeds.

4. Remove the cake barrel from the air fryer, and pour out any accumulated liquid from the partially cooked cabbage. Pour the dressing mixture over the drained cabbage and mix well. Return the bowl to the air fryer and cook for 7 to 11 minutes more, stirring twice during cooking time, until the cabbage is tender and the sauce has thickened.

LOVING YOUR LEFTOVERS If you have any leftovers from this recipe, heat in the air fryer with some sliced cooked sausages for a great fast lunch. If you really love mustard, eat with some Dijon mustard on the side.

Indian-Inspired Roasted Bell Peppers

30-MINUTE, GLUTEN-FREE, VEGAN

SERVES 4

PREP TIME
15 minutes

COOK TIME
15 minutes, plus
10 minutes to steam

PREHEAT
375°F

PER SERVING
Calories: 38
Total fat: 0g
Saturated fat: 0g
Cholesterol: 0mg
Sodium: 294mg
Carbohydrates: 8g
Fiber: 2g
Protein: 1g

When bell peppers are roasted, they become tender and taste very sweet, the perfect foil for Indian spices. The peppers are roasted whole so the skin chars, then put in a paper bag to steam. The skin is peeled off to reveal the luscious flesh. Use multicolored peppers in this beautiful dish.

1 red bell pepper

1 orange bell pepper

1 yellow bell pepper

2 teaspoons curry powder

1 tablespoon fresh lemon juice

½ teaspoon salt

1. Rinse the peppers and dry them off. Pierce each with a fork a few times.

2. Set or preheat the air fryer to 375°F. Place the peppers in the air fryer basket. Cook for 12 to 15 minutes, shaking the basket halfway through cooking time, until the pepper skins are wrinkled and browned in spots.

3. Remove the peppers from the air fryer and place them in a brown paper bag. Let stand for 10 minutes to steam.

4. Remove the skin from the peppers, cut them in half, and remove the stems and seeds. Slice the peppers, then sprinkle with the curry powder, lemon juice, and salt before serving.

INGREDIENT TIP Never rinse a roasted pepper when you peel it, because rinsing removes the flavor compounds that are developed during cooking. Instead, remove as much skin as you can with your fingers.

Shrimp Scampi, page 89

CHAPTER 5
FISH AND SHELLFISH

Shrimp Fried Rice

FAMILY FAVORITE

Full of texture and flavor, shrimp fried rice is a classic Asian recipe. For best results, start with cold cooked rice. Aim to make this when you have leftover rice, or use frozen cooked rice that's been thawed. You can add any veggie you want to this delicious recipe.

1 pound medium shrimp, peeled and deveined

1 small onion, chopped

2 garlic cloves, minced

1 tablespoon olive oil

1 tablespoon butter

2 large eggs, beaten

2 cups cold cooked rice

1 cup frozen baby peas, thawed

2 tablespoons reduced-sodium soy sauce

1 tablespoon oyster sauce

1. In a cake barrel, combine the shrimp, onion, garlic, and olive oil.

2. Set or preheat the air fryer to 375°F. Place the cake barrel in the air fryer. Cook the shrimp mixture for 5 to 7 minutes, stirring once during the cooking time, until the shrimp curl and turn pink. Remove from the cake barrel and set aside in a bowl.

3. Place the butter in the hot cake barrel and let it melt, then add the eggs to the hot pan and return to the air fryer. Cook for 4 to 6 minutes, stirring once, until the eggs are set. Remove the eggs from the pan and set aside.

4. Add the rice, peas, soy sauce, and oyster sauce to the cake barrel and return it to the air fryer. Cook for 12 to 15 minutes, stirring once halfway through the cooking time, until the rice is hot and starting to crisp.

5. Add the shrimp mixture and eggs to the cake barrel and stir. Cook for another 2 to 3 minutes or until everything is hot.

INGREDIENT TIP If you make rice ahead of time for this recipe, be sure to store it in the refrigerator. Otherwise, you risk food poisoning. Rice can contain bacterial spores that will survive cooking and grow unless it's kept chilled.

California Fish Tacos

SERVES 4

PREP TIME
15 minutes

COOK TIME
15 minutes

PREHEAT
350°F

PER SERVING
Calories: 539
Total fat: 29g
Saturated fat: 8g
Cholesterol: 71mg
Sodium: 911mg
Carbohydrates: 44g
Fiber: 12g
Protein: 30g

This recipe features several ingredients that showcase the flavors of California, including fish fillets, orange juice, and avocado. This fun variation on a taco is easy to make, fresh, and delicious. Your family will love it.

1 lemon, thinly sliced

16 ounces red snapper or halibut fish fillets

1 tablespoon olive oil

1 tablespoon chili powder

½ teaspoon salt

2 cups shredded coleslaw mix with carrots

2 tablespoons orange juice

½ cup salsa

4 (10-inch) flour tortillas

½ cup sour cream

2 avocados, sliced

1. Arrange the lemon slices in the bottom of the air fryer basket.

2. Set or preheat the air fryer to 350°F. Drizzle the fish fillets with the olive oil and sprinkle with the chili powder and salt. Put the fillets on top of the lemons in the air fryer basket. Cook for 6 to 9 minutes or until the fish flakes when tested with a fork.

3. Meanwhile, in a bowl, toss together the coleslaw mix, orange juice, and salsa.

4. Once the fish is done, remove it from the air fryer basket and cover to keep warm. Discard the lemons.

5. To warm the tortillas, wrap the tortillas in foil and put them in the air fryer basket. Cook for 2 to 3 minutes or until the tortillas are warm.

6. To make the tacos, put the fish in the tortillas and top with the cabbage mixture, sour cream, and avocados.

SPICE IT UP You can make these tacos as spicy as you'd like. Add a minced jalapeño or chipotle pepper in adobo to the coleslaw mix, and sprinkle the fish fillets with ¼ teaspoon cayenne pepper before cooking.

FRY FACT Most fish taco recipes call for deep-fried fish. This recipe is healthier because the fish is roasted to perfection in the air fryer.

Salmon en Papillote

FAMILY FAVORITE, GLUTEN-FREE

SERVES 4

PREP TIME
15 minutes

COOK TIME
28 minutes

PREHEAT
400°F

PER SERVING
Calories: 252
Total fat: 13g
Saturated fat: 5g
Cholesterol: 78mg
Sodium: 417mg
Carbohydrates: 9g
Fiber: 3g
Protein: 23g

Papillote is the French word for "foil"; to cook en papillote simply means to cook food enclosed in foil. This method of cooking seals in the juices and flavor and results in tender and moist salmon. And, yes, you can use parchment paper in the air fryer. This elegant dish is perfect for company or an everyday meal.

1 orange, sliced

4 salmon fillets

1 teaspoon dried thyme

½ teaspoon sea salt

⅛ teaspoon freshly ground black pepper

1 cup shredded carrots

1 red bell pepper, thinly sliced

½ cup sliced celery

2 tablespoons butter

1. Preheat the oven to 250°F.

2. Tear off four 15-inch lengths of parchment paper, and fold each piece in half crosswise. Place the orange slices in the center of one half of each piece of paper, and top with the salmon. Sprinkle each fillet with the thyme, sea salt, and black pepper. Top each salmon fillet with one-quarter of the carrots, bell pepper, and celery, and dot with the butter.

3. Fold the parchment paper in half and crimp the edges all around to enclose the salmon and vegetables.

4. Set or preheat the air fryer to 400°F. Put one of the parchment bundles in the basket, add a raised rack, and top with one more bundle. Cook for 12 to 14 minutes or until the parchment paper bundles puff up. The salmon should just flake with a fork when you test it. Put the cooked bundles in the oven to keep them warm.

5. Cook the second batch of parchment bundles.

6. When serving, be aware that hot steam will be released when the bundles are opened.

LOVING YOUR LEFTOVERS   If you have leftovers, put the remaining salmon and vegetables atop some leafy greens in a bowl. Finish with your favorite salad dressing.

Coconut Shrimp

FAMILY FAVORITE, GLUTEN-FREE

SERVES 4

PREP TIME
15 minutes

COOK TIME
24 minutes

PREHEAT
380°F

PER SERVING
Calories: 409
Total fat: 15g
Saturated fat: 11g
Cholesterol: 186mg
Sodium: 1,232mg
Carbohydrates: 49g
Fiber: 3g
Protein: 23g

A classic deep-fried recipe, coconut shrimp cook beautifully in the air fryer. This easy recipe is ready in minutes. The shrimp are tender, the coating is crisp, and the dipping sauce is sweet and hot.

1¼ pounds large shrimp, peeled and deveined, tails on

¼ cup cornstarch or coconut flour

1 teaspoon salt

⅛ teaspoon freshly ground black pepper

2 egg whites

1½ cups unsweetened shredded coconut

⅔ cup pineapple or apricot jam

¼ cup sour cream

2 tablespoons Dijon mustard

1 tablespoon fresh lemon juice

Pinch cayenne pepper

1. Pat the shrimp dry and set aside.

2. Combine the cornstarch, salt, and pepper on a plate. In a shallow bowl, beat the egg whites until frothy. Spread the shredded coconut on another plate.

3. One at a time, dip the shrimp in the cornstarch mixture, then the egg whites, and then the shredded coconut. Place the coated coconut shrimp on a wire rack as you work.

4. Set or preheat the air fryer to 380°F. Place as many shrimp as will fit in a single layer in the air fryer basket. Cook for 5 minutes, then carefully turn the shrimp and cook for 3 to 7 minutes more or until the shrimp curl and the coconut browns. Repeat with remaining shrimp.

5. Meanwhile, in a small bowl, combine the pineapple jam, sour cream, mustard, lemon juice, and cayenne to make the dipping sauce.

6. Serve the shrimp with the dipping sauce.

INGREDIENT TIP Shrimp size is determined by how many there are in a pound. Small shrimp are about 55 per pound; medium, 45 per pound; large, 31 per pound; and jumbo, 21 per pound. You want shrimp that are about 31 per pound for this recipe.

Crisp Salmon Nuggets *with* Green Sauce

SERVES 4

PREP TIME
15 minutes

COOK TIME
24 minutes

PREHEAT
400°F

PER SERVING
Calories: 400
Total fat: 19g
Saturated fat: 4g
Cholesterol: 72mg
Sodium: 877mg
Carbohydrates: 25g
Fiber: 3g
Protein: 32g

In this delicious recipe, a salmon fillet is cut into pieces, coated with panko bread crumbs, and air-fried until crisp and tender. The green sauce is made with … broccoli! The cruciferous vegetable makes a suave, flavorful sauce. A vegetable-based sauce is a great way to get more veggies in your diet.

1½ cups frozen broccoli florets

3 garlic cloves, peeled

3 tablespoons sour cream

2 tablespoons fresh lemon juice

2 tablespoons olive oil

1 teaspoon sea salt, divided

2 egg whites

1 cup panko bread crumbs

¼ cup grated Parmesan cheese

1 teaspoon dried basil

⅛ teaspoon freshly ground black pepper

1 pound center-cut salmon fillet, cut into 1½-inch cubes

Cooking oil, for misting

1. Set or preheat the air fryer to 400°F. Put the broccoli and garlic in the air fryer basket. Cook for 5 to 7 minutes or until tender.

2. Transfer the broccoli and garlic to a blender or food processor and add the sour cream, lemon juice, olive oil, and ½ teaspoon of salt and process until smooth. Set the sauce aside.

3. Put the egg whites in a shallow bowl and beat until frothy. Combine the panko, Parmesan, basil, pepper, and the remaining ½ teaspoon of salt on a plate. Dip the salmon in the egg whites and then the bread crumbs, pressing to coat.

4. Set or preheat the air fryer to 400°F. Arrange half of the salmon cubes in the air fryer basket and mist with cooking oil. Cook for 6 to 8 minutes or until the salmon is just cooked through, rearranging once during that time.

5. Repeat with the second batch of salmon.

6. Serve the salmon with the sauce.

MAKE IT A MEAL Serve this recipe with a side of Honey-Roasted Baby Carrots (page 63) and Lemon Bars (page 154) for dessert. Add a fruit salad and a nice glass of white wine.

Shrimp Risotto

FAMILY FAVORITE, GLUTEN-FREE

SERVES 4

PREP TIME
15 minutes

COOK TIME
35 minutes, plus
5 minutes to stand

PREHEAT
380°F

PER SERVING
Calories: 440
Total fat: 16g
Saturated fat: 6g
Cholesterol: 135mg
Sodium: 1,135mg
Carbohydrates: 50g
Fiber: 3g
Protein: 22g

Risotto is an elegant Italian recipe that uses short-grain Arborio rice to create a creamy and delicious main dish. To make it the traditional way, you have to stand at the stove, stirring constantly. Not with the air fryer. Shrimp is the perfect addition to this classic dish.

2 tablespoons olive oil, divided

1 pound medium shrimp, peeled and deveined

1 onion, finely chopped

1 red bell pepper, chopped

½ teaspoon sea salt

⅛ teaspoon freshly ground black pepper

1 cup Arborio rice

2⅓ cups chicken stock or vegetable broth

2 tablespoons butter

⅓ cup grated Parmesan cheese

1. Put 1 tablespoon of olive oil in a cake barrel, then add the shrimp.

2. Set or preheat the air fryer to 380°F. Place the cake barrel in the air fryer basket. Cook the shrimp for 4 to 7 minutes or until they curl and turn pink. Remove the shrimp from the cake barrel and set aside.

3. Add the remaining 1 tablespoon of olive oil to the cake barrel, along with the onion, bell pepper, salt, and black pepper. Cook for 3 minutes.

4. Add the rice to the cake barrel, stir, and cook for 2 minutes. Then, add the chicken stock, stir again, and cover the cake barrel with foil. Cook for another 18 to 22 minutes or until the rice is tender, stirring twice during the cooking time. Remove the foil.

5. Return the shrimp to the cake barrel along with the butter and Parmesan. Cook for 1 minute more.

6. Remove from the air fryer, cover with foil again, and let stand for 5 minutes. Stir and serve.

INGREDIENT TIP Short-grain rice is used for making risotto because its starch content helps to make a creamy sauce. The starch is released while the rice is cooking. Arborio is the classic rice type used in risotto and the best choice for this recipe.

Shrimp *and* Crab Cakes

SERVES 4

PREP TIME
15 minutes

COOK TIME
15 minutes

PREHEAT
375°F

PER SERVING
Calories: 230
Total fat: 14g
Saturated fat: 2g
Cholesterol: 114mg
Sodium: 643mg
Carbohydrates: 14g
Fiber: 2g
Protein: 13g

What's one way to improve delicious crab cakes? Add some chopped cooked shrimp. The combination of textures and flavors in this recipe is excellent. Seafood lovers will gobble them up.

1 cup lump crabmeat

1 cup chopped cooked shrimp

3 scallions, finely chopped

1 egg, beaten

¼ cup mayonnaise

2 tablespoons honey mustard

¾ cup saltine cracker crumbs, divided

1 tablespoon fresh lemon juice

Cooking oil, for misting

Nonstick cooking spray

1. In a medium bowl, combine the crabmeat, shrimp, scallions, egg, mayonnaise, honey mustard, ¼ cup of cracker crumbs, and the lemon juice; mix gently.

2. Form into 4 patties. Sprinkle with the remaining ½ cup of cracker crumbs on both sides. Mist with cooking oil.

3. Set or preheat the air fryer to 375°F.

4. Line the air fryer basket with a round of parchment paper that has holes punched into it. Coat the paper with cooking spray. Put the patties on the parchment paper. Cook for 10 to 14 minutes or until the patties are set and golden brown.

MAKE IT A MEAL   Add a green salad topped with mushrooms and tomatoes, and serve the cakes with a sauce made from ½ cup mayonnaise, 2 tablespoons mustard, 2 tablespoons sweet pickle relish, and ⅛ teaspoon cayenne pepper. Baked potatoes on the side would be delicious.

Parmesan Garlic Shrimp

30-MINUTE, FAMILY FAVORITE, GLUTEN-FREE

SERVES 4

———

PREP TIME
5 minutes

———

COOK TIME
10 minutes

———

PREHEAT
350°F

———

PER SERVING
Calories: 187
Total fat: 8g
Saturated fat: 3g
Cholesterol: 189mg
Sodium: 928mg
Carbohydrates: 4g
Fiber: 0g
Protein: 23g

A classic Mediterranean combination gets the air-fryer treatment in this irresistible dish. Tender shrimp is encased in Parmesan cheese that turns crisp in the air fryer heat, and garlic adds the right flavor.

1¼ pounds large shrimp, peeled and deveined

1 tablespoon olive oil

1 tablespoon fresh lemon juice

½ teaspoon garlic powder

2 garlic cloves, minced

½ cup grated Parmesan cheese

1. Put the shrimp in a large bowl and sprinkle with the olive oil, lemon juice, and garlic powder. Add the minced garlic and Parmesan, and toss to coat.

2. Set or preheat to the air fryer to 350°F. Place the shrimp in the air fryer basket. Cook the shrimp for 8 to 12 minutes, shaking the basket once during the cooking time, until the shrimp curl and turn pink.

SPICE IT UP   You can make this recipe spicy by adding ⅛ to ¼ teaspoon cayenne pepper to the Parmesan cheese before you coat the shrimp. Or, sprinkle the shrimp with a bit of red pepper flakes before serving.

Classic Fish 'n' Chips

FAMILY FAVORITE

SERVES 4

PREP TIME
15 minutes

COOK TIME
25 minutes

PREHEAT
400°F

PER SERVING
(WITHOUT
TARTAR SAUCE)
Calories: 462
Total fat: 11g
Saturated fat: 2g
Cholesterol: 102mg
Sodium: 783mg
Carbohydrates: 59g
Fiber: 4g
Protein: 31g

This British dish is found in pubs all over the United Kingdom, and it is famous the world over. The combination of crisp fries (the Brits call them chips) and moist and crunchy fish is the ultimate comfort food, especially when there's a creamy tartar sauce for dipping.

2 russet potatoes, peeled

2 tablespoons olive oil

1 teaspoon sea salt, divided

4 fish fillets (4 to 6 ounces each)

¼ cup all-purpose flour

⅛ teaspoon freshly ground black pepper

1 teaspoon Old Bay seasoning

1 egg, beaten

1 cup panko bread crumbs

Cooking oil, for misting

Tartar sauce or ketchup, for serving

1. Preheat the oven to 250°F. Set a wire rack on a baking sheet.

2. Cut the potatoes into ½-inch-thick fries (or chips), and drizzle with the olive oil. Sprinkle with ½ teaspoon of salt.

3. Set or preheat the air fryer to 400°F. Put the fries in the air fryer basket and cook for 12 to 16 minutes, shaking the basket once during cooking time, until the fries are crisp and golden. Put them on the rack on the baking sheet, and transfer to the oven to keep warm.

4. Sprinkle the fish fillets with the remaining ½ teaspoon of salt. Season the flour with the pepper and Old Bay seasoning and spread on a plate. Put the egg in a shallow bowl. Spread the panko on another plate.

5. Dip the fish in the flour, then the egg, and then the panko, pressing to coat.

CONTINUED

6. Put half the fish in the air fryer basket and mist with cooking oil. Add a raised rack to the air fryer basket, top with the remaining fish, and mist with cooking oil. Cook for 8 to 10 minutes or until the fish flakes when tested with a fork.

7. Serve the fish and chips with tartar sauce or ketchup.

INGREDIENT TIP   Old Bay seasoning is a classic spice mix for seafood. If you don't want to buy it just for one recipe, make your own: Combine ¼ teaspoon celery salt, ¼ teaspoon paprika, ⅛ teaspoon mustard powder, ⅛ teaspoon cayenne pepper, ⅛ teaspoon freshly ground black pepper, and ⅛ teaspoon nutmeg. Store what you don't use for later.

FRY FACT   This recipe is much healthier and much crunchier than the classic deep-fried fish 'n' chips.

English Muffin Crab Pizzas

30-MINUTE, FAMILY FAVORITE

MAKES 8 PIZZAS

———

PREP TIME
10 minutes

———

COOK TIME
15 minutes

———

PREHEAT
400°F

———

PER SERVING
(1 PIZZA)
Calories: 334
Total fat: 23g
Saturated fat: 11g
Cholesterol: 98mg
Sodium: 507mg
Carbohydrates: 33g
Fiber: 4g
Protein: 17g

English muffins are a great base for pizza. The muffins stand up to the topping and don't collapse or get soggy. This luscious combination of crab and cheese is reminiscent of your favorite party dip, but it's served on a crispy pizza.

8 ounces cream cheese, at room temperature

¼ cup mayonnaise

¼ cup seafood cocktail sauce

1 tablespoon fresh lemon juice

12 ounces lump crabmeat

3 scallions, chopped

4 English muffins

2 tablespoons butter

1 cup shredded Gruyère cheese

1. In a medium bowl, combine the cream cheese and mayonnaise and beat until smooth. Stir in the cocktail sauce and lemon juice. Stir in the crabmeat and scallions.

2. Split the English muffins in half with a fork. Spread with the butter.

3. Set or preheat the air fryer to 400°F. Place 4 muffin halves in the air fryer basket. Top with a rack and add the remaining 4 muffin halves. Cook the English muffins for 3 minutes, then remove them from the air fryer.

4. Divide the crab filling among the English muffins, and top with the Gruyère. Put the pizzas back in the air fryer, using the rack again. Bake for 6 to 10 minutes or until the pizzas are hot and starting to brown on top.

> **FRY TIP** If you have an oven-style air fryer, you may be able to fit all the pizzas on a rack in a single layer. If you have a small basket-type air fryer, you may need to cook the pizzas in two batches.

Lemony Sea Scallops

30-MINUTE, FAMILY FAVORITE, GLUTEN-FREE

SERVES 4

PREP TIME
5 minutes

COOK TIME
10 minutes

PREHEAT
400°F

PER SERVING
Calories: 149
Total fat: 7g
Saturated fat: 1g
Cholesterol: 15mg
Sodium: 336mg
Carbohydrates: 1g
Fiber: 0g
Protein: 21g

Scallops are bivalves—like clams or mussels—but what we eat is not the animal that lives in the shell, but rather the muscle used to open and close the shell. This is why scallops are so meaty. Four sea scallops are one serving, although this lemony version is so tasty that you may want to offer six scallops per person.

16 to 24 sea scallops

½ teaspoon sea salt

⅛ teaspoon freshly ground black pepper

2 tablespoons butter, melted

1 teaspoon grated lemon zest

2 tablespoons fresh lemon juice

1. Pat the scallops dry with paper towels, then sprinkle with the salt and pepper. Place in a medium bowl.

2. In a small bowl, combine the melted butter, lemon zest, and lemon juice; mix well. Drizzle half of this mixture over the scallops.

3. Set or preheat the air fryer to 400°F. Put the scallops in the air fryer basket. Cook for 8 to 11 minutes, turning the scallops over halfway during the cooking time, until they are opaque. The internal temperature should be 145°F.

4. Remove the scallops to a serving bowl and drizzle with the remaining lemon mixture.

INGREDIENT TIP There are two kinds of scallops: sea and bay. Sea scallops are much larger than bay scallops. There's an easy way to remember this: The sea is larger than a bay, so sea scallops are bigger. If you can only find bay scallops, cook them for 3 to 5 minutes or until opaque. If there is a little muscle attached to the side of the scallop, pull it off and discard it before cooking, since it is too tough to eat.

Shrimp Scampi

30-MINUTE, FAMILY FAVORITE, GLUTEN-FREE

SERVES 4

———

PREP TIME
10 minutes

———

COOK TIME
15 minutes

———

PREHEAT
400°F

———

PER SERVING
(WITHOUT PASTA
OR RICE)
Calories: 296
Total fat: 21g
Saturated fat: 7g
Cholesterol: 237mg
Sodium: 1,115mg
Carbohydrates: 4g
Fiber: 0g
Protein: 24g

Shrimp scampi is a crowd-pleaser. Make this recipe for a casual weeknight dinner, or double it and let it be the hit of the party. The combination of lemon, garlic, and shrimp is irresistible.

1½ **pounds medium shrimp, peeled and deveined**

6 garlic cloves, minced

1 teaspoon salt

¼ **teaspoon lemon pepper seasoning**

½ **teaspoon grated lemon zest**

3 tablespoons fresh lemon juice

3 tablespoons olive oil

3 tablespoons butter

2 teaspoons fresh thyme leaves

Cooked pasta or rice, for serving

1. In a cake barrel, combine the shrimp and garlic. Sprinkle with the salt and lemon pepper seasoning and toss to coat. Add the lemon zest, lemon juice, olive oil, and butter.

2. Set or preheat the air fryer to 400°F. Place the cake barrel in the air fryer basket. Cook the shrimp for 5 minutes, then stir. Cook for another 5 to 8 minutes or until the shrimp curl and turn pink. Sprinkle with the thyme.

3. Serve over hot cooked pasta or rice.

INGREDIENT TIP You can buy shrimp that have been deveined, but if yours aren't, just cut a shallow slit along the back side of the shrimp. You'll see a dark line that you need to remove with your fingers or rinse out.

MAKE IT A MEAL Serve this shrimp with a green salad and Garlicky Green Beans (page 66) or Honey-Roasted Baby Carrots (page 63).

Fish Po'Boys

SERVES 4

PREP TIME
15 minutes

COOK TIME
15 minutes

PREHEAT
375°F

PER SERVING
Calories: 536
Total fat: 33g
Saturated fat: 8g
Cholesterol: 80mg
Sodium: 926mg
Carbohydrates: 35g
Fiber: 3g
Protein: 25g

A po'boy (or poor boy) is a classic treat from Louisiana. The sandwich is usually stuffed with meat or seafood and served on a fluffy white French bread bun. Po'boys typically contain shrimp, but you can use any type of seafood.

1 pound white fish fillets

½ teaspoon sea salt

2 tablespoons buttermilk

2 tablespoons fresh lemon juice

1 tablespoon olive oil

½ cup dried bread crumbs

2 teaspoons spice mix from Cajun Shrimp Boil (page 91), divided

½ cup mayonnaise

4 French bread hoagie buns, split

2 tablespoons butter, at room temperature

2 tomatoes, cut into ½-inch-thick slices

8 leaves butter lettuce

1. Sprinkle the fish with the salt. Cut the fish into 2-inch pieces, and place them in a medium bowl. Add the buttermilk, lemon juice, and olive oil; let stand for 10 minutes while you prepare the remaining ingredients.

2. Put the bread crumbs on a plate, and mix with 1 teaspoon of the Cajun shrimp boil spice mix. Remove the fish pieces from the buttermilk mixture, and coat them with the bread crumb mixture. Place in the air fryer basket. Discard the buttermilk mixture.

3. Set or preheat the air fryer to 375°F. Cook the fish for 8 to 11 minutes, rearranging the fish with tongs halfway through the cooking time, until the fish flakes when tested with a fork.

4. Combine the remaining 1 teaspoon spice mix with the mayonnaise. Spread the buns with the butter, and make sandwiches with the fish, mayonnaise mixture, tomatoes, and butter lettuce.

SUBSTITUTION TIP You can use shrimp or freshly shucked oysters in place of the fish. Butterfly the shrimp (cut them almost in half lengthwise, then open them up like books). Cook the shrimp for 4 to 5 minutes, until they are firm, and cook the oysters for 3 to 4 minutes or until firm.

Cajun Shrimp Boil

GLUTEN-FREE

SERVES 4

———

PREP TIME
10 minutes

———

COOK TIME
26 minutes

———

PREHEAT
375°F

———

PER SERVING
Calories: 304
Total fat: 6g
Saturated fat: 1g
Cholesterol: 143mg
Sodium: 546mg
Carbohydrates: 44g
Fiber: 7g
Protein: 22g

Cajun cooking—from the Acadian region of Louisiana, with French influences—is represented in this spice mix, which has kick but also a depth of flavor from the dried herbs and paprika. Shrimp is especially tasty when coated with this mix and cooked in the air fryer with corn and potatoes.

1 tablespoon smoked paprika

2 teaspoons dried thyme

1 teaspoon dried marjoram

1 teaspoon sea salt

1 teaspoon garlic powder

1 teaspoon onion powder

1 teaspoon cayenne pepper

1 pound baby Yukon Gold potatoes, halved

8 frozen "mini" corn on the cob

1 tablespoon olive oil

1 pound large shrimp, peeled and deveined

1. For the spice mix: In a bowl, combine the paprika, thyme, marjoram, salt, garlic powder, onion powder, and cayenne; mix well. Transfer to a small, screw-top glass jar. (Some of the spice mix is used in this recipe; save the rest for other uses. Store at room temperature.)

2. Set or preheat the air fryer to 375°F. Combine the potatoes, corn, and olive oil in the air fryer basket. Sprinkle with 2 teaspoons of the spice mix and toss. Cook the potatoes and corn for 15 minutes, shaking the basket halfway through cooking time, until they are tender. Remove from the basket and set aside.

3. Add the shrimp to the air fryer basket and sprinkle with 2 teaspoons of the spice mix. Cook for 5 to 8 minutes, shaking the basket once, until the shrimp are tender and turn pink.

4. Now, combine all the ingredients in the air fryer basket and sprinkle with another 2 teaspoons of the spice mix; toss. Cook for 1 to 2 minutes or until hot, then serve.

SUBSTITUTION TIP You can add some fully cooked smoked sausage to this recipe if you'd like. Just slice it and cook along with the shrimp.

Sriracha Tuna Melt

30-MINUTE

SERVES 4

PREP TIME
10 minutes

COOK TIME
10 minutes

PREHEAT
375°F

PER SERVING
Calories: 425
Total fat: 29g
Saturated fat: 11g
Cholesterol: 77mg
Sodium: 588mg
Carbohydrates: 16g
Fiber: 3g
Protein: 26g

A tuna melt is a classic open-faced diner sandwich—in other words, no lid. Spicy sriracha, a hot sauce made from chiles, garlic, and vinegar, really wakes up a tuna melt. You can omit it if you don't like really spicy food, or substitute a milder hot sauce, such as Tabasco.

2 whole wheat English muffins

2 tablespoons butter, at room temperature

1 (12-ounce) can light tuna, drained

⅓ cup mayonnaise

2 tablespoons Dijon mustard

1 tablespoon fresh lemon juice

⅓ cup chopped celery

½ teaspoon sriracha sauce

4 slices tomato

4 slices Swiss cheese

1. Split the English muffins with a fork. Spread each of the 4 halves with the butter.

2. Set or preheat the air fryer to 375°F. Put the muffin halves in the air fryer basket and cook for 3 to 5 minutes or until toasted. Remove from the air fryer and set aside.

3. In a medium bowl, combine the tuna, mayonnaise, mustard, lemon juice, celery, and sriracha; mix gently. Divide among the English muffin halves.

4. Top each of the sandwiches with a tomato slice and a cheese slice. Place in the air fryer basket. Cook for 4 to 6 minutes or until the cheese is melted and starts to brown.

SUBSTITUTION TIP You can use any seafood in this sandwich recipe. Try using canned crab or salmon in place of the tuna. And you can use 4 slices of toasted bread in place of the English muffin halves.

Shrimp *and* Pineapple Kebabs

FAMILY FAVORITE, GLUTEN-FREE

SERVES 4

PREP TIME
15 minutes, plus
30 minutes to soak

COOK TIME
10 minutes

PREHEAT
375°F

PER SERVING
Calories: 191
Total fat: 5g
Saturated fat: 1g
Cholesterol: 214mg
Sodium: 832mg
Carbohydrates: 12g
Fiber: 2g
Protein: 24g

Shrimp kebabs are easy to make and fun to eat. This texture, color, and flavor contrast from the shrimp and pineapple gets a boost from a bit of spice. Use bamboo skewers in this recipe; soak them in water for 30 minutes before using so they don't burn in the air fryer.

1½ pounds large shrimp, peeled and deveined

1 (8-ounce) can pineapple chunks, drained, liquid reserved

1 red bell pepper, cut into 1½-inch pieces

3 scallions, cut into 1-inch pieces

1 tablespoon fresh lemon juice

1 tablespoon olive oil

½ teaspoon sea salt

⅛ teaspoon cayenne pepper

1. Thread the shrimp, pineapple, bell pepper pieces, and scallions onto 8 soaked bamboo skewers.

2. In a small bowl, mix 3 tablespoons reserved pineapple juice with the lemon juice, olive oil, salt, and cayenne pepper. Brush this mixture onto the threaded skewers, using all the marinade.

3. Set or preheat the air fryer to 375°F. Put 4 kebabs in the air fryer basket. Add a raised rack and add the remaining 4 skewers. (If you don't have a rack, cook the skewers in batches). Cook for 6 to 9 minutes, rearranging the skewers halfway through cooking time, until the shrimp curl and turn pink.

MAKE IT A MEAL Add some crusty rolls and a green salad tossed with tomatoes and cucumbers to complete this meal. For dessert, make Buckeye Brownies (page 148) or Vanilla Wafer Cupcakes (page 146).

Classic Fried Chicken, page 104

CHAPTER 6
POULTRY

Bacon-Wrapped Chicken Tenders

FAMILY FAVORITE, GLUTEN-FREE

SERVES 4

PREP TIME
15 minutes

COOK TIME
20 minutes

PREHEAT
375°F

PER SERVING
Calories: 352
Total fat: 21g
Saturated fat: 6g
Cholesterol: 108mg
Sodium: 560mg
Carbohydrates: 7g
Fiber: 0g
Protein: 32g

Bacon adds fabulous flavor and a crunchy texture to this easy chicken recipe. The bacon gets crisp as the chicken cooks to tender perfection. You can buy chicken tenders at the grocery store; they are sometimes labeled chicken tenderloins—just be sure to purchase the ones without breading.

¼ **cup mayonnaise**

¼ **cup plain Greek yogurt**

3 **tablespoons ketchup**

1 **tablespoon yellow mustard**

1 **tablespoon light brown sugar**

1 **pound chicken tenders (tenderloins)**

1 **teaspoon dried thyme**

8 to 10 **bacon slices**

1. In a small bowl, combine the mayonnaise, yogurt, ketchup, mustard, and brown sugar and mix well. Set the sauce aside.

2. Sprinkle the chicken with the thyme and wrap each one in a slice of bacon.

3. Set or preheat the air fryer to 375°F. Arrange the wrapped chicken in the air fryer basket in a single layer. If necessary, add a raised rack and put half of the tenders on the rack. Cook the tenders for 10 minutes, then flip and cook for another 8 to 10 minutes or until the chicken reads 165°F on a food thermometer and the bacon is crisp. Serve with the sauce.

SUBSTITUTION TIP If you can't find chicken tenders in your grocery store, you can substitute 2 boneless, skinless chicken breasts. Cut each breast into 4 thin strips and proceed with the recipe.

Chicken Parm Hoagies

30-MINUTE, FAMILY FAVORITE

SERVES 4

PREP TIME
15 minutes

COOK TIME
11 minutes

PREHEAT
370°F

PER SERVING
Calories: 484
Total fat: 17g
Saturated fat: 7g
Cholesterol: 190mg
Sodium: 865mg
Carbohydrates: 38g
Fiber: 3g
Protein: 44g

This recipe takes chicken Parmesan, a classic Italian recipe, and puts it inside a hoagie roll for a casual and delicious dish. Serve with more marinara sauce on the side.

2 boneless, skinless chicken breasts (8 ounces each)

1 teaspoon Italian seasoning

½ teaspoon sea salt

1 egg

1 egg yolk

2 tablespoons water

½ cup panko bread crumbs

½ cup grated Parmesan cheese

Cooking oil, for misting

1 cup shredded mozzarella cheese

4 hoagie rolls, split and toasted

1½ cups marinara sauce, heated on the stovetop

1. Halve each chicken breast horizontally to make cutlets. Put the chicken cutlets between two sheets of parchment paper and pound until they are about ¼ inch thick. Sprinkle with the Italian seasoning and salt.

2. Put the whole egg and egg yolk in a shallow bowl and beat with the water. Put the panko and Parmesan onto a plate and mix.

3. Dip the chicken cutlets in the egg mixture, then the panko mixture, pressing to coat. Place on a wire rack to stand for 10 minutes.

4. Set or preheat the air fryer to 370°F. Put 2 chicken cutlets in the air fryer basket and mist with cooking oil. Add a raised rack and add the second 2 cutlets and mist with cooking oil. Cook the chicken for 8 to 11 minutes or until the chicken reads 165°F on a food thermometer (see Tip). Remove the rack with the chicken and then top all cutlets ¼ cup mozzarella. Let stand until melted.

5. Put the bottoms of the hoagie buns on the work surface. Spread each with 3 tablespoons of marinara sauce. Top with the chicken, 3 tablespoons marinara, then the top half of the buns.

INGREDIENT TIP To get an accurate temperature reading, insert the tip of the probe into the side of the chicken.

Orange Chicken *and* Snap Peas

30-MINUTE, FAMILY FAVORITE, GLUTEN-FREE

SERVES 4

PREP TIME
10 minutes

COOK TIME
15 minutes

PREHEAT
375°F

PER SERVING
Calories: 278
Total fat: 2g
Saturated fat: 0g
Cholesterol: 65mg
Sodium: 643mg
Carbohydrates: 38g
Fiber: 1g
Protein: 27g

Orange chicken, a favorite at American Chinese restaurants, is traditionally made by coating deep-fried chicken breast in a tangy orange sauce. It's easy to make this recipe in the air fryer, and the results are spectacular. Serve with hot cooked rice and some fresh fruit.

2 boneless, skinless chicken breasts (8 ounces each)

½ teaspoon sea salt

⅛ teaspoon freshly ground black pepper

6 tablespoons cornstarch, divided

1 cup orange juice

¼ cup orange marmalade

¼ cup ketchup

½ teaspoon ground ginger

2 tablespoons reduced-sodium gluten-free soy sauce

1⅓ cups snap peas

1. Cut the chicken breasts into 1-inch pieces and sprinkle with the salt and pepper. Coat the chicken with 4 tablespoons of cornstarch and put on a wire rack to set while you prepare the sauce.

2. In a cake barrel, combine the orange juice, marmalade, ketchup, ginger, soy sauce, and remaining 2 tablespoons of cornstarch. Stir in the snap peas.

3. Set or preheat the air fryer to 375°F. Put the cake barrel in the air fryer basket. Cook for 5 to 8 minutes, stirring once during cooking time, until the sauce is bubbling and thickened. Remove the cake barrel from the air fryer and set aside.

4. Add the chicken to the air fryer basket. Cook for 10 to 12 minutes, shaking the basket once during cooking time, until the chicken reads 165°F on a food thermometer.

5. Add the chicken to the sauce and snap peas in the cake barrel and stir gently. Return to the basket. Cook for another 1 to 2 minutes or until the sauce is hot.

SPICE IT UP   This recipe is traditionally mild, but you can certainly spice things up. Sprinkle the chicken with cayenne pepper instead of black pepper, and add a minced jalapeño pepper to the sauce.

Sesame Chicken

FAMILY FAVORITE, GLUTEN-FREE

SERVES 4

PREP TIME
15 minutes

COOK TIME
20 minutes

PREHEAT
400°F

PER SERVING
Calories: 299
Total fat: 9g
Saturated fat: 2g
Cholesterol: 148mg
Sodium: 703mg
Carbohydrates: 21g
Fiber: 1g
Protein: 34g

Sesame chicken is another favorite at Chinese American restaurants. Chicken thighs are cooked until crisp, then coated in a rich, fragrant sauce. The whole thing is sprinkled with sesame seeds for crunch. It's so much better than takeout.

1½ pounds boneless, skinless chicken thighs

3 tablespoons reduced-sodium gluten-free soy sauce, divided

3 tablespoons apple cider vinegar, divided

½ teaspoon ground ginger

⅛ teaspoon freshly ground black pepper

6 tablespoons cornstarch, divided

1 cup chicken stock

2 tablespoons hoisin sauce

2 tablespoons light brown sugar

2 tablespoons toasted sesame seeds

1. Cube the chicken thighs and put them in a cake barrel. Add 1 tablespoon of soy sauce, 1 tablespoon of vinegar, the ground ginger, and the pepper. Mix and let stand for 10 minutes.

2. Remove the chicken from the marinade, then coat it in 4 tablespoons of cornstarch. Let stand while you prepare the sauce.

3. To the marinade remaining in the cake barrel, add the chicken stock, hoisin sauce, brown sugar, and remaining 2 tablespoons of soy sauce, 2 tablespoons of vinegar, and 2 tablespoons of cornstarch; mix well.

4. Set or preheat the air fryer to 400°F. Place the cake barrel in the air fryer basket. Cook the sauce for 5 to 8 minutes or until bubbling and thickened, stirring once during the cooking time. Remove the cake barrel from the air fryer basket and set aside.

5. Add the chicken to the air fryer basket. Cook for 15 to 18 minutes, tossing the chicken in the basket once during the cooking time, until the chicken reads 165°F on a food thermometer.

6. Add the chicken to the sauce in the cake barrel, and return the barrel to the air fryer. Cook for 1 to 2 minutes more or until everything is hot. Sprinkle with the sesame seeds and serve.

MAKE IT A MEAL   Serve over hot cooked rice with Roasted Garlic Brussels Sprouts (page 57) or Stir-Fried Zucchini and Yellow Squash (page 68) on the side. Add some fruit to your plate, too, for some cooling contrast.

Hasselback Chicken

FAMILY FAVORITE

SERVES 4

PREP TIME
15 minutes

COOK TIME
20 minutes

PREHEAT
350°F

PER SERVING
Calories: 524
Total fat: 33g
Saturated fat: 14g
Cholesterol: 139mg
Sodium: 833mg
Carbohydrates: 21g
Fiber: 3g
Protein: 35g

Hasselback potatoes are cut so individual potato slices fan out from the larger potato as it cooks (try Hasselback Fingerling Potatoes, page 55). The same technique can be used on chicken. For this recipe, stuff the breasts with a creamy spinach mixture and tomato slices, then top them with bread crumbs for a crisp finish.

1 (8-ounce) package cream cheese, at room temperature

6 tablespoons grated Parmesan cheese, divided

1 cup frozen cut-leaf spinach, thawed and squeezed dry

1 teaspoon dried thyme

4 boneless, skinless chicken breasts (6 ounces each)

½ teaspoon salt

⅛ teaspoon freshly ground black pepper

3 small tomatoes, sliced into ¼-inch-thick rounds (24 total slices)

⅓ cup creamy ranch salad dressing

⅔ cup panko bread crumbs

Cooking oil, for misting

1. In a small bowl, combine the cream cheese, 2 tablespoons of Parmesan, the spinach, and thyme; mix well. Set aside.

2. Cut 6 vertical slices in each chicken breast, being careful not to cut through to the bottom, making 6 pockets in each breast. Sprinkle the chicken with the salt and pepper.

3. Divide the cream cheese mixture among the pockets in the chicken breasts, smearing about 1 teaspoon inside each one. Place a tomato slice in each pocket. Brush the chicken with the salad dressing, and sprinkle with the panko.

4. Set or preheat the air fryer to 350°F. Place the chicken in a single layer in the air fryer basket. Mist the chicken with some cooking oil. (You may need to cook the chicken in batches if you have a smaller air fryer.)

5. Cook for 15 to 20 minutes or until the chicken registers 165°F on a food thermometer.

Curried Chicken Nuggets

30-MINUTE

SERVES 4

PREP TIME
10 minutes

COOK TIME
18 minutes

PREHEAT
400°F

PER SERVING
Calories: 426
Total fat: 22g
Saturated fat: 7g
Cholesterol: 136mg
Sodium: 612mg
Carbohydrates: 24g
Fiber: 3g
Protein: 32g

Chicken nuggets cook beautifully in the air fryer. But why not take them to the next level? Curry powder and a dipping sauce made from mango chutney really spice up this nostalgic classic food.

1 pound boneless, skinless chicken breasts

4 teaspoons curry powder, divided

½ teaspoon sea salt

⅛ teaspoon freshly ground black pepper

1 egg, beaten

2 tablespoons butter, melted

1 cup panko bread crumbs

Cooking oil, for misting

½ cup plain Greek yogurt

⅓ cup mango chutney

¼ cup mayonnaise

1. Cut the chicken into 1-inch pieces. Sprinkle with 3 teaspoons of curry powder, the salt, and the pepper; toss to coat.

2. In a shallow bowl, beat together the egg and melted butter. Put the panko on a plate. Dip the chicken pieces in the egg mixture, then the panko, pressing to coat. Put the coated nuggets on a wire rack as you work.

3. Set or preheat the air fryer to 400°F. Put half of the nuggets in the air fryer and mist with cooking oil. Cook for 7 to 9 minutes, rearranging the nuggets with tongs halfway through cooking time, until the chicken reads 165°F on a food thermometer.

4. Repeat with remaining half of chicken nuggets.

5. Meanwhile, in a small bowl, combine the yogurt, chutney, mayonnaise, and remaining 1 teaspoon of curry powder.

6. Serve the nuggets with the dipping sauce.

MAKE IT A MEAL   Serve these nuggets with Garlicky Green Beans (page 66) or Apples 'n' Onions (page 71) for a great meal. A small green salad completes the dinner.

Classic Fried Chicken

FAMILY FAVORITE

SERVES 4

PREP TIME
10 minutes,
plus 15 minutes
to marinate

COOK TIME
45 minutes

PREHEAT
375°F

PER SERVING
Calories: 538
Total fat: 36g
Saturated fat: 10g
Cholesterol: 175mg
Sodium: 476mg
Carbohydrates: 13g
Fiber: 1g
Protein: 44g

Fried chicken cooks to perfection in the air fryer, and with none of the mess and fuss of deep-frying. The secret to this Southern classic is in the breading mix, which is highly seasoned for great flavor. You can marinate the chicken overnight, but 15 minutes is also fine.

2 cups all-purpose flour

4 teaspoons salt

4 teaspoons dried basil

4 teaspoons dried thyme

2 teaspoons dried marjoram

2 teaspoons smoked paprika

1 teaspoon mustard powder

1 teaspoon celery salt

1 cup buttermilk

¼ cup honey

1 whole chicken (about 3 pounds), cut into breasts, drumsticks, and thighs

Cooking oil, for misting

1. For the breading mix: In a small bowl, mix together the flour, salt, basil, thyme, marjoram, paprika, mustard powder, and celery salt. Transfer the breading mix to a screw-top glass jar. (Some of the breading mix is used in this recipe; save the rest for other uses. Store at room temperature.)

2. In a large bowl, combine the buttermilk and honey and mix well. Add the chicken pieces and stir to coat. Let stand for 15 minutes at room temperature, or cover and marinate overnight in the refrigerator.

3. When you're ready to cook, preheat the oven to 250°F and remove the chicken from the buttermilk mixture. Discard the buttermilk mixture.

4. Put ⅔ cup of the breading mix on a plate. Dip the chicken pieces in the mix, pressing to coat. Shake the chicken gently, then put the chicken on a wire rack as you work. Let the coated chicken stand for 10 minutes.

5. Set or preheat the air fryer to 375°F. Line the air fryer basket with a round of parchment paper that has holes punched into it. Put half of the chicken pieces in the basket in a single layer. Mist with cooking oil.

6. Cook the chicken for 18 to 23 minutes, turning once halfway through the cooking time and misting with more oil, until it reads 165°F on a food thermometer. Put the cooked chicken in the oven to keep warm.

7. Repeat with remaining chicken, using a fresh round of parchment paper.

INGREDIENT TIP   So as not to contaminate the breading mix with bacteria from the chicken, remove ⅔ cup of the breading mixture from the jar with a measuring cup. Never dip fingers that have touched chicken in the reserved breading mix, or you will introduce pathogens.

FRY FACT   Air-fried chicken is not only healthier, but also crispier than deep-fried chicken.

Sweet *and* Sour Chicken

FAMILY FAVORITE

SERVES 4

PREP TIME
15 minutes

COOK TIME
15 minutes

PREHEAT
400°F

PER SERVING
Calories: 322
Total fat: 3g
Saturated fat: 1g
Cholesterol: 97mg
Sodium: 427mg
Carbohydrates: 32g
Fiber: 2g
Protein: 39g

Sweet and sour chicken is a classic Asian-inspired dish that is usually stir-fried. This air fryer version couldn't be easier to make, and it has just as much flavor as the original. Serve over hot cooked rice or quinoa for a great meal.

1½ pounds boneless, skinless chicken breasts

4 tablespoons cornstarch, divided

⅛ teaspoon freshly ground black pepper

1 (8-ounce) can pineapple tidbits, drained, ¼ cup juice reserved

1 cup chicken stock

¼ cup packed light brown sugar

⅓ cup apple cider vinegar

2 tablespoons ketchup

2 tablespoons reduced-sodium soy sauce

1 red bell pepper, chopped

1. Cut the chicken into 1-inch pieces. Sprinkle with 2 tablespoons of cornstarch and the pepper and toss to coat.

2. Set or preheat the air fryer to 400°F. Put the chicken in the air fryer basket. Cook the chicken for 7 to 9 minutes, shaking the basket once during the cooking time, until the chicken is almost cooked.

3. In a cake barrel, whisk together the remaining 2 tablespoons of cornstarch, ¼ cup reserved pineapple juice, stock, brown sugar, vinegar, ketchup, and soy sauce.

4. Add the cooked chicken, bell pepper, and pineapple tidbits to the cake barrel. Put the barrel in the air fryer basket and cook for 7 to 10 minutes, stirring once halfway through cooking time, until the sauce is thickened, the bell peppers are crisp-tender, and the chicken reads 165°F on a food thermometer.

SUBSTITUTION TIP You can substitute cubes of pork or chicken thighs for the chicken breasts in this recipe. The pork will cook in the same time; add another 2 minutes for the chicken thighs in step 3. If you can't eat gluten, make sure the soy sauce is gluten-free, or use gluten-free tamari.

Turkey Breast *with* Berry Glaze

FAMILY FAVORITE, GLUTEN-FREE

SERVES 4

PREP TIME
10 minutes

COOK TIME
1 hour 5 minutes,
plus 10 minutes
to stand

PREHEAT
350°F

PER SERVING
Calories: 824
Total fat: 41g
Saturated fat: 13g
Cholesterol: 310mg
Sodium: 739mg
Carbohydrates: 7g
Fiber: 3g
Protein: 100g

A turkey breast is the perfect size for a larger air fryer. This easy recipe frees up your oven for a bigger bird on Thanksgiving, and it's a great way to cook turkey in the summer. The berry glaze is sweet and tart, thanks to the honey mustard.

1 bone-in, skin-on turkey breast (about 4 pounds)

1 tablespoon olive oil

1 teaspoon sea salt

⅛ teaspoon freshly ground black pepper

1 cup raspberries

1 cup chopped strawberries

2 tablespoons fresh lemon juice

2 tablespoons butter, melted

1 tablespoon honey mustard

1. Set or preheat the air fryer to 350°F. Put the turkey breast skin-side up in the air fryer basket; brush with the oil and sprinkle with the salt and pepper. Cook the turkey for 25 minutes, then turn the breast on one side and cook for another 15 minutes. Finally, turn the breast to the other side and cook for another 15 to 20 minutes or until the turkey reads 165°F on a food thermometer.

2. Meanwhile, in a blender or food processor, combine the raspberries, strawberries, lemon juice, melted butter, and honey mustard; process until smooth.

3. Turn the turkey skin-side up again in the air fryer basket. Brush about half of the berry mixture over the cooked turkey. Cook for another 5 to 6 minutes or until the glaze has set.

4. While the turkey is finishing, put the remaining berry mixture in a small saucepan and simmer for 3 to 4 minutes.

5. Let the turkey breast stand for 10 minutes, then carve. Serve the turkey with the remaining glaze.

FRY FACT When buying the turkey breast, make sure that it will fit in your air fryer basket with a little room to spare. You could get a boneless turkey breast to save room; the cooking time will decrease to about 50 minutes total.

Classic Roast Chicken

FAMILY FAVORITE, GLUTEN-FREE

SERVES 4

PREP TIME
10 minutes

COOK TIME
55 minutes, plus
10 minutes to stand

PREHEAT
350°F

PER SERVING
Calories: 545
Total fat: 40g
Saturated fat: 14g
Cholesterol: 188mg
Sodium: 207mg
Carbohydrates: 1g
Fiber: 0g
Protein: 42g

Everybody loves roast chicken, and for good reason. The skin gets crisp, the meat is tender and juicy, and the flavor is out of this world. Make sure that the chicken you buy will fit in your air fryer.

1 whole roasting chicken (3 to 5 pounds)

2 tablespoons butter, at room temperature

2 tablespoons breading mix from Classic Fried Chicken (page 104)

1 lemon

1. Remove the giblets from the chicken and freeze for later use. Pat the chicken dry; don't rinse it, or you could spray bacteria around your kitchen.

2. Loosen the skin on the chicken breasts, and rub half of the butter under the skin. Smooth the skin back over the chicken and secure it with toothpicks. Rub the remaining butter on the outside of the bird.

3. Sprinkle the bird with 1 tablespoon of the breading mix, rubbing it in to make sure the spices adhere.

4. Pressing down, roll the lemon on the kitchen counter with your hands. Cut the lemon in half, and put both halves inside the chicken. If you can't fit both in, keep the other half for another use, as long as it hasn't touched the raw chicken.

5. Set or preheat the air fryer to 350°F. Line the bottom of the air fryer basket with a round of parchment paper with holes punched into it. Put the chicken in the air fryer basket, breast-side down. Cook the chicken for 30 minutes, then remove it from the air fryer and turn it breast-side up. Cook for another 15 to 25 minutes or until the chicken reads 165°F on a food thermometer.

6. Put the chicken on a serving plate and cover with foil. Let stand for 10 minutes, then carve to serve.

MAKE IT A MEAL Classic sides for this delicious recipe include Honey-Roasted Baby Carrots (page 63), Twice-Baked Potatoes (page 56), and Dill-Roasted Carrots and Parsnips (page 60).

Turkey Spinach Meatballs

FAMILY FAVORITE

SERVES 4

PREP TIME
15 minutes

COOK TIME
30 minutes

PREHEAT
400°F

PER SERVING
Calories: 295
Total fat: 14g
Saturated fat: 4g
Cholesterol: 150mg
Sodium: 583mg
Carbohydrates: 8g
Fiber: 2g
Protein: 34g

Meatballs made with turkey are more tender and juicy than those made with beef. They also have fewer calories and less fat. The spinach, onion, and marjoram in this recipe impart a punch of flavor. You can add these meatballs to pasta sauce to serve over spaghetti, or use them to make meatball sandwiches.

2 scallions, finely chopped

1 garlic clove, minced

1 egg, beaten

1 cup frozen cut-leaf spinach, thawed and squeezed dry

¼ cup dried bread crumbs

¼ cup grated Parmesan cheese

1 teaspoon dried marjoram

½ teaspoon sea salt

⅛ teaspoon finely ground black pepper

1¼ pounds ground turkey (dark and light meat)

1. Preheat the oven to 250°F.

2. In a medium bowl, combine the scallions, garlic, egg, spinach, bread crumbs, Parmesan, marjoram, salt, and pepper; mix well. Add the turkey and mix gently but thoroughly. Form into 1½-inch balls.

3. Set or preheat the air fryer to 400°F. Arrange as many meatballs as can fit in a single layer in the air fryer basket. Cook the meatballs for 10 to 15 minutes, gently shaking the basket halfway through cooking time, until the meatballs read 165°F on a food thermometer. Put the cooked meatballs on a tray in the oven and cover with foil to keep warm.

4. Repeat with the remaining meatballs.

INGREDIENT TIP All ground poultry needs to be cooked to 165°F for food safety reasons. All ground meat—beef, lamb, veal, and pork—needs to be cooked to 160°F. Make sure you have an accurate food thermometer.

Turkey French Bread Pizza

FAMILY FAVORITE

SERVES 4

PREP TIME
20 minutes

COOK TIME
15 minutes

PREHEAT
375°F

PER SERVING
Calories: 617
Total fat: 34g
Saturated fat: 18g
Cholesterol: 126mg
Sodium: 1,521mg
Carbohydrates: 40g
Fiber: 5g
Protein: 37g

French bread halves make a great base for a pizza topped with turkey sausage and veggies. The bread gets crunchy and airy when air fried, and it highlights the flavorful toppings.

1 (12-inch) loaf French bread

2 tablespoons butter, at room temperature

1 teaspoon garlic powder

1⅓ cups pizza sauce

1 teaspoon Italian seasoning

10 fully cooked turkey sausages, sliced

2 scallions, chopped

1 red bell pepper, chopped

1 cup shredded mozzarella cheese

1 cup shredded Cheddar cheese

1. Cut the loaf of French bread in half crosswise, then split each half horizontally.

2. In a small bowl, mix together the butter and garlic powder. Spread on the cut sides of the bread.

3. Set or preheat the air fryer to 375°F. Put the bread halves in the air fryer. Cook for 3 to 5 minutes or until the loaves start to brown on top. You may need to do this in batches.

4. Put the toasted bread halves on a work surface and spread with the pizza sauce. Sprinkle with the Italian seasoning and top with the sausage slices, scallions, bell pepper, and both cheeses.

5. Put the pizzas back in the air fryer. You may need to do this in batches. Cook for 8 to 12 minutes or until the pizzas are hot and the cheese has melted and starts to brown.

MAKE IT A MEAL Serve this pizza with a green salad tossed with mushrooms and cherry tomatoes. Finish with Carrot Cake (page 157) or Roasted Pear Tart (page 159) for dessert.

INGREDIENT TIP If you can't find fully cooked turkey sausages, buy uncooked ones. Prick each with a fork, put them in the air fryer, and cook for about 20 minutes at 375°F or until the sausages register 160°F on a food thermometer.

Bacon Chicken Drumsticks

FAMILY FAVORITE, GLUTEN-FREE

SERVES 4

PREP TIME
10 minutes

COOK TIME
30 minutes

PREHEAT
350°F

PER SERVING
Calories: 410
Total fat: 23g
Saturated fat: 7g
Cholesterol: 179mg
Sodium: 589mg
Carbohydrates: 8g
Fiber: 0g
Protein: 38g

For this recipe to work, you must remove the skin from the drumsticks. Brown sugar, ketchup, and mustard add a wonderful flavor, as does the bacon.

8 chicken drumsticks

2 tablespoons light brown sugar

2 tablespoons ketchup

1 tablespoon Dijon mustard

8 bacon slices

1. Remove the skin from the drumsticks: Using a paper towel, grasp the skin and pull it away from the meat and bones. Discard the skins.

2. In a small bowl, mix together the brown sugar, ketchup, and mustard.

3. Brush the chicken with some of the brown sugar mixture, then wrap a slice of bacon around each drumstick. Brush with the remaining brown sugar mixture.

4. Set or preheat the air fryer to 350°F. Line the air fryer basket with a round of parchment paper with holes punched into it. Put 4 of the drumsticks on the paper, then add a raised rack and the remaining 4 drumsticks. Cook the drumsticks for 25 to 35 minutes, turning them over and rearranging them from top to bottom halfway through the cooking time. When done, the drumsticks should register 165°F on a food thermometer and the bacon should be cooked.

SUBSTITUTION TIP You can use this method with bone-in skinless chicken thighs as well. The cook time will be 22 to 27 minutes; just make sure to cook them to 165°F.

Parmesan Chicken Tenders

30-MINUTE, FAMILY FAVORITE, GLUTEN-FREE

SERVES 4

PREP TIME
10 minutes

COOK TIME
15 minutes

PREHEAT
400°F

PER SERVING
Calories: 255
Total fat: 9g
Saturated fat: 4g
Cholesterol: 163mg
Sodium: 537mg
Carbohydrates: 3g
Fiber: 0g
Protein: 38g

Chicken tenders are versatile, and kids love them. These tenders are coated in grated and shredded Parmesan cheese for a wonderful texture. Serve them with marinara sauce or blue cheese salad dressing for dipping, or use them in sandwiches.

1¼ pounds chicken tenders (tenderloins)

1 egg, beaten

2 tablespoons 2% milk

½ teaspoon sea salt

⅛ teaspoon freshly ground black pepper

½ teaspoon garlic powder

¼ teaspoon onion powder

⅓ cup grated Parmesan cheese

¼ cup shredded Parmesan cheese

Cooking oil, for misting

1. Pat the chicken tenders dry.

2. In a shallow bowl, stir together the egg and milk. Combine the salt, pepper, garlic powder, onion powder, and both types of Parmesan on a plate.

3. One at a time, dip the chicken tenders in the egg mixture and then the cheese mixture, pressing to coat. Place them on a wire rack as you work.

4. Set or preheat the air fryer to 400°F. Arrange as many tenders in the air fryer basket as will fit in a single layer. Use a raised rack to cook more at one time. Mist the tenders with oil. Cook for 12 to 16 minutes, turning the chicken over halfway through the cooking time, until the meat registers 165°F on a food thermometer.

SUBSTITUTION TIP You can use this technique with boneless, skinless chicken breasts; the cooking time will increase to 20 to 25 minutes.

Tex-Mex Turkey Burgers

FAMILY FAVORITE

SERVES 4

———

PREP TIME
15 minutes

———

COOK TIME
20 minutes

———

PREHEAT
375°F

———

PER SERVING
Calories: 557
Total fat: 32g
Saturated fat: 11g
Cholesterol: 169mg
Sodium: 882mg
Carbohydrates: 25g
Fiber: 2g
Protein: 41g

Turkey burgers make a nice change from the classic beef burger. These are spicy, flavored with several types of chiles. Serve them on toasted hamburger buns with guacamole, sour cream, and salsa.

½ cup salsa, divided

1 large egg, beaten

3 garlic cloves, minced

1 jalapeño pepper, minced

½ teaspoon sea salt

⅛ teaspoon freshly ground black pepper

1¼ pounds ground turkey

¼ cup mayonnaise

4 onion buns, split and toasted

4 slices pepper Jack cheese

4 large slices tomato

1. In a large bowl, combine ¼ cup of salsa, the egg, garlic, jalapeño, salt, and black pepper and mix well. Add the turkey and mix gently but thoroughly. Form into 4 patties.

2. Set or preheat the air fryer to 375°F. Put the patties in the air fryer basket, preferably on a grill pan if you have one. Cook for 17 to 22 minutes or until the burgers are 165°F on a food thermometer.

3. Meanwhile, in a small bowl, combine the mayonnaise and remaining ¼ cup of salsa.

4. When the burgers are done, spread some of the mayonnaise mixture on the bottom half of the buns. Top with the cooked turkey burgers, pepper Jack cheese, tomatoes, and more of the mayonnaise mixture, then add the tops of the buns.

SPICE IT UP If you like things spicy, use two jalapeño peppers and cayenne pepper in place of the black pepper. Choose your favorite spicy salsa.

Chicken Salad *with* Roasted Grapes

FAMILY FAVORITE, GLUTEN-FREE

SERVES 4

PREP TIME
20 minutes

COOK TIME
20 minutes

PREHEAT
375°F

PER SERVING
Calories: 373
Total fat: 24g
Saturated fat: 4g
Cholesterol: 78mg
Sodium: 627mg
Carbohydrates: 18g
Fiber: 2g
Protein: 22g

This classic chicken salad is made with grapes and celery. When the chicken is cooked in the air fryer, it comes out tender and juicy. The grapes are roasted, too, so they add sweetness. You can eat this salad right away, or chill it in the refrigerator first.

3 boneless, skinless chicken breasts

1 teaspoon paprika

½ teaspoon salt

⅛ teaspoon freshly ground black pepper

2 cups seedless red grapes

½ cup mayonnaise

½ cup plain yogurt

2 tablespoons honey mustard

2 tablespoons fresh lemon juice

1 cup chopped celery

2 scallions, chopped

1. Pat the chicken dry with paper towels. Sprinkle with the paprika, salt, and pepper.

2. Set or preheat the air fryer to 375°F. Put the chicken in the air fryer basket. Cook the chicken for 16 to 19 minutes, flipping the chicken halfway through the cooking time, until the chicken reads 165°F on a food thermometer.

3. Remove the chicken to a cutting board and let stand.

4. Put the grapes in the air fryer basket and mist with cooking oil. Cook for 3 to 4 minutes or until the grapes are hot and tender.

5. In a large bowl, combine the mayonnaise, yogurt, honey mustard, and lemon juice and whisk until combined.

6. Cube the chicken and add to the dressing, along with the grapes, celery, and scallions. Toss gently and serve, or chill for a few hours in the refrigerator.

LOVING YOUR LEFTOVERS Leftover chicken salad is a wonderful thing. You can eat it as is, or put it on toasted bread, flatbread, or English muffins for a great lunch.

Spanish-Inspired Chicken Kebabs

FAMILY FAVORITE, GLUTEN-FREE

SERVES 4

PREP TIME
15 minutes, plus
30 minutes to soak

COOK TIME
20 minutes

PREHEAT
400°F

PER SERVING
Calories: 224
Total fat: 12g
Saturated fat: 2g
Cholesterol: 64mg
Sodium: 471mg
Carbohydrates: 8g
Fiber: 3g
Protein: 21g

The flavors of Spain—smoked paprika, roasted red peppers, olive oil, olives, garlic, and onions—flavor the chicken breasts and veggies for a great twist on classic kebabs. To prevent them from burning, soak the skewers in water for 30 minutes before you start the recipe.

3 boneless, skinless chicken breasts

¼ cup plain yogurt

2 tablespoons olive oil

1 teaspoon smoked paprika

1 teaspoon dried oregano

½ teaspoon sea salt

½ teaspoon garlic powder

2 red bell peppers

3 scallions

1 yellow summer squash, sliced

16 large green olives

1. Soak 8 (6-inch) bamboo skewers in water for 30 minutes.

2. Meanwhile, pat the chicken dry with paper towels. Cut into 1½-inch pieces.

3. In a medium bowl, combine the yogurt, olive oil, smoked paprika, oregano, salt, and garlic powder. Add the chicken and stir to coat. Let stand while you prepare the remaining ingredients.

4. Cut the bell peppers and scallions into 1-inch pieces.

5. Remove the chicken from the marinade, reserving the marinade. Thread the chicken, peppers, scallions, squash, and olives onto the soaked skewers. Brush the kebabs with the marinade. Discard any remaining marinade.

6. Set or preheat the air fryer to 400°F. Put 4 kebabs in the air fryer basket. Add a raised rack and add the remaining 4 skewers. (If you don't have a rack, cook in batches.) Cook for 18 to 23 minutes, flipping the kebabs halfway through, until the chicken registers 165°F on a food thermometer.

FRY FACT If you can find metal skewers that will fit in your air fryer, use those. Even with soaking, bamboo skewers will burn a bit during this longer cooking time.

Herbed Turkey Tenderloins

FAMILY FAVORITE, GLUTEN-FREE

SERVES 4

PREP TIME
10 minutes

COOK TIME
25 minutes

PREHEAT
350°F

PER SERVING
Calories: 252
Total fat: 10g
Saturated fat: 2g
Cholesterol: 114mg
Sodium: 672mg
Carbohydrates: 1g
Fiber: 0g
Protein: 37g

Turkey tenderloin is a nice cut of meat. It has little fat, cooks quickly and evenly, and there's no waste. The fresh herb marinade in this recipe adds lots of fabulous flavor.

**2 turkey tenderloins
(12 ounces each)**

2 tablespoons olive oil

1 teaspoon salt

**⅛ teaspoon freshly ground
black pepper**

**2 tablespoons minced
fresh parsley**

**1 tablespoon minced fresh
thyme leaves**

**1 tablespoon minced fresh
basil leaves**

1. Rub the turkey tenderloins with the olive oil and sprinkle with the salt and pepper. Add the parsley, thyme, and basil; and rub the seasoning mixture all over the meat.

2. Set or preheat the air fryer to 350°F. Put the tenderloins in the air fryer basket with a bit of space between them. Cook for 22 to 27 minutes, flipping the turkey halfway through the cooking time, until the turkey reads 165°F on a food thermometer.

3. Put the turkey onto a serving plate, cover with foil, and let stand for 5 minutes before slicing to serve.

MAKE IT A MEAL Serve this recipe with Mediterranean Roasted Cherry Tomatoes (page 69) and Potatoes au Gratin (page 59). For dessert, try Fried Ice Cream (page 145).

Steak Fajitas, page 126

CHAPTER 7
BEEF, PORK, AND LAMB

Swedish Meatballs

FAMILY FAVORITE

SERVES 4

PREP TIME
20 minutes

COOK TIME
25 minutes

PREHEAT
350°F

PER SERVING
Calories: 356
Total fat: 22g
Saturated fat: 10g
Cholesterol: 147mg
Sodium: 187mg
Carbohydrates: 12g
Fiber: 1g
Protein: 27g

These meatballs are seasoned with onion and garlic and a little nutmeg. Sour cream is used in the sauce and is also added to the meatballs.

1 tablespoon olive oil

1 small onion, diced

2 garlic cloves, minced

Pinch nutmeg

¼ cup soft fresh bread crumbs

½ cup sour cream, divided

1 egg yolk

1 pound lean ground beef

2 tablespoons butter, melted

3 tablespoons all-purpose flour

1½ cups beef broth

1. In a cake barrel, combine the olive oil, onion, and garlic.

2. Set or preheat the air fryer to 350°F. Put the barrel in the air fryer. Cook for 3 to 4 minutes or until the vegetables are crisp-tender.

3. Transfer the veggies to a bowl (set aside the cake barrel). Add the nutmeg, bread crumbs, ¼ cup of sour cream, and the egg yolk to the veggies and mix well. Add the beef and mix by hand. Form into 1-inch meatballs.

4. Set or preheat the air fryer to 350°F. Place the meatballs in the air fryer basket. Cook for 10 to 15 minutes, rearranging the meatballs halfway through the cooking time, until the meatballs read 160°F on a food thermometer. Remove the meatballs and set aside.

5. In the cake barrel, combine the melted butter and flour. Put in the air fryer basket and cook for 2 minutes. Add the beef broth and whisk, then cook for 4 minutes or until thickened.

6. Quickly whisk the remaining ¼ cup of sour cream into the sauce, then add the meatballs. Cook for another 2 to 3 minutes or until the sauce is bubbling. Serve hot.

MAKE IT A MEAL Serve this recipe over mashed potatoes, hot cooked rice, or egg noodles. Add Garlicky Green Beans (page 66) and Lemon Bars (page 154) to round out the meal.

Sausage *and* Potatoes Tray Bake

FAMILY FAVORITE, GLUTEN-FREE

SERVES 4

────────

PREP TIME
15 minutes

────────

COOK TIME
25 minutes

────────

PREHEAT
375°F

────────

PER SERVING
Calories: 547
Total fat: 40g
Saturated fat: 12g
Cholesterol: 66mg
Sodium: 1,244mg
Carbohydrates: 30g
Fiber: 5g
Protein: 18g

Tray bakes are an easy way to get dinner on the table in a hurry. They are truly one-dish meals. You can add a green salad if you'd like. The sausages, veggies, and potatoes in this recipe get a pop of flavor from the honey mustard drizzle.

1 pound baby Yukon Gold potatoes, halved

1 cup halved Brussels sprouts

1 cup baby carrots

1 onion, sliced

2 tablespoons olive oil

½ teaspoon sea salt

⅛ teaspoon freshly ground black pepper

1 pound fully cooked smoked sausages, sliced

2 tablespoons honey mustard

1. Set or preheat the air fryer to 375°F. Put the potatoes, Brussels sprouts, baby carrots, and onion in the air fryer basket. Drizzle with the olive oil, sprinkle with the salt and pepper, and toss to coat.

2. Cook the veggies for 15 minutes or until they are crisp-tender, shaking the basket once during the cooking time.

3. Add the sausages to the air fryer basket. Cook for another 8 to 12 minutes, shaking the basket once during the cooking time, until the sausages are hot and the veggies are tender.

4. Place everything on a serving dish and drizzle with the honey mustard. Serve.

SUBSTITUTION TIP   When Brussels sprouts are roasted, they become quite sweet and lose much of their bitterness. If you don't like Brussels sprouts, use green beans or broccoli instead.

Pork Medallions *in* Mustard Sauce

30-MINUTE, FAMILY FAVORITE, GLUTEN-FREE

SERVES 4

PREP TIME
10 minutes

COOK TIME
15 minutes

PREHEAT
350°F

PER SERVING
Calories: 259
Total fat: 16g
Saturated fat: 9g
Cholesterol: 116mg
Sodium: 519mg
Carbohydrates: 3g
Fiber: 1g
Protein: 25g

These pork medallions are pounded until thin, which makes them tender, then bathed in a creamy, garlic-scented mustard sauce.

1 pound pork tenderloin

½ teaspoon sea salt

⅛ teaspoon freshly ground black pepper

½ teaspoon dried marjoram

2 tablespoons butter

1 tablespoon garlic-flavored olive oil

1 small onion, diced

1 cup chicken stock

2 tablespoons Dijon mustard

2 tablespoons grainy mustard

⅓ cup heavy (whipping) cream

1. Slice the pork tenderloin crosswise into ½-inch-thick rounds. Place the rounds, cut-side down, between sheets of parchment paper, then pound them with a rolling pin until they are about ¼ inch thick.

2. Sprinkle the pork with the salt, pepper, and marjoram.

3. Set or preheat the air fryer to 350°F. Arrange the pork in the air fryer basket. Cook for 5 to 8 minutes or until the medallions are almost cooked. Remove the pork from the basket and wipe out the basket.

4. In a cake barrel, combine the butter, garlic oil, onion, and chicken stock. Set the barrel in the air fryer basket. Cook for 4 to 5 minutes or until the onions are crisp-tender.

5. Add the two types of mustard and the cream to the barrel. Cook for 4 minutes or until the mixture starts to thicken.

6. Add the pork medallions to the sauce in the cake barrel, and cook for 3 to 5 minutes or until the sauce begins to simmer.

SPICE IT UP Although this recipe is typically mild, you can add spices if you'd like. Add some cayenne pepper or red pepper flakes in place of the black pepper, or add some horseradish to the mustard mixture.

Bagel Pizzas

30-MINUTE, FAMILY FAVORITE

SERVES 4

PREP TIME
10 minutes

COOK TIME
10 minutes

PREHEAT
375°F

PER SERVING
Calories: 466
Total fat: 21g
Saturated fat: 10g
Cholesterol: 76mg
Sodium: 986mg
Carbohydrates: 44g
Fiber: 3g
Protein: 25g

Sliced bagels make an excellent base for pizza. Choose your favorite bagel for this easy recipe. If you'd prefer more room for toppings, scoop out some of the inside of the bagel and save it for bread crumbs. Just don't poke a hole through the bagel, or the filling will leak.

2 large bagels, halved horizontally

1 (8-ounce) can pizza sauce

⅓ cup sliced pepperoni

2 scallions, chopped

2 cups shredded mozzarella cheese

¼ cup grated Parmesan cheese

2 tablespoons minced fresh chives

1. Set or preheat the air fryer to 375°F. Put the bagel halves, cut side up, in the air fryer basket. Cook for 2 to 3 minutes, until light golden brown.

2. Remove the bagels from the basket and top them with the pizza sauce, pepperoni, scallions, and both cheeses.

3. Return the bagels, topping-side up, to the air fryer basket. Cook for 8 to 12 minutes or until the bagels are hot and the cheese has melted and is starting to bubble and brown.

4. Top with the chives and serve.

SUBSTITUTION TIP Play with different cooked meats, types of sauce, and kinds of cheese. Try using leftover cooked sausage, sliced cooked pork, leftover ground beef, Cheddar cheese, and Swiss cheese.

Southwest Burgers

SERVES 4

PREP TIME
15 minutes

COOK TIME
14 minutes

PREHEAT
375°F

PER SERVING
Calories: 493
Total fat: 22g
Saturated fat: 11g
Cholesterol: 123mg
Sodium: 606mg
Carbohydrates: 31g
Fiber: 2g
Protein: 44g

Burgers cook beautifully in the air fryer, whether you have a grill pan (for those pretty grill marks) or not. This recipe gets a jolt from Southwest seasonings, including chipotles in adobo, chili powder, and pepper Jack cheese.

¼ cup soft fresh bread crumbs

2 tablespoons 2% milk

1 chipotle pepper in adobo sauce, minced

6 tablespoons salsa, divided

2 teaspoons chili powder

2 tablespoons grated Cotija or Parmesan cheese

1¼ pounds lean ground beef

4 slices pepper Jack cheese

¼ cup sour cream

4 onion buns, split and toasted

1. In a medium bowl, combine the bread crumbs, milk, chipotle pepper, 2 tablespoons of salsa, the chili powder, and Cotija cheese; mix well. Let stand for 5 minutes.

2. Add the ground beef to the bread crumb mixture, and mix gently but thoroughly with your hands. Form into 4 patties about ½ inch thick. Place the patties on wax paper.

3. Set or preheat the air fryer to 375°F. Turn the patties over using the wax paper, and drop them on a grill pan in the air fryer basket, or place them directly in the air fryer basket, removing the paper. You may need to do this in batches.

4. Cook the burgers for 11 to 14 minutes, turning the burgers with a spatula halfway through the cooking time, until a food thermometer inserted in the side of a burger registers 160°F.

5. Put a slice of pepper Jack on top of each burger, and cook for another minute or until the cheese melts.

6. Meanwhile, in a small bowl, combine the remaining 4 tablespoons of salsa with the sour cream.

7. Spread the bun bottoms with some of the sour cream mixture, top with the burgers, and spoon the rest of the sour cream mixture on the patties. Add the tops of the buns and serve.

SPICE IT UP   Rev up this burger with some guacamole, or add sliced tomatoes and lettuce. For even more spice, add a second chipotle pepper and replace the 2 tablespoons of salsa with adobo sauce.

FRY FACT   Cook ground beef to 160°F, especially if you have a person in your household who is at risk for food poisoning complications.

Steak Fajitas

30-MINUTE, FAMILY FAVORITE, GLUTEN-FREE

SERVES 4

PREP TIME
15 minutes

COOK TIME
15 minutes

PREHEAT
400°F

PER SERVING
Calories: 533
Total fat: 26g
Saturated fat: 12g
Cholesterol: 124mg
Sodium: 713mg
Carbohydrates: 31g
Fiber: 5g
Protein: 45g

Fajitas are a fun party food. You just pile the food on a platter, and everyone makes their own plate. This recipe excels in the air fryer because you can cook the steak and veggies together. Add additional toppings such as chopped cilantro, guacamole, or chopped avocados drizzled with lime juice.

1¼ pounds flank steak, cut against the grain into ½-inch-thick strips

½ teaspoon sea salt

⅛ teaspoon freshly ground black pepper

2 tablespoons fresh lime juice

4 garlic cloves, minced

2 teaspoons chili powder

1 red bell pepper, sliced

1 yellow bell pepper, sliced

1 tablespoon olive oil

½ cup salsa

1½ cups shredded Colby or pepper Jack cheese

8 corn tortillas

1. Put the steak in a medium bowl and sprinkle with the sea salt, pepper, lime juice, garlic, and chili powder; toss well. Let stand while you prepare the remaining ingredients.

2. Set or preheat the air fryer to 400°F. Combine the bell peppers with the olive oil in the air fryer basket and toss. Cook the peppers for 5 to 6 minutes, until crisp-tender.

3. Drain the flank steak, discarding the liquid. Add the steak slices to the basket on top of the peppers. Cook for 7 to 9 minutes more or until the steak registers at least 145°F on a meat thermometer.

4. To assemble the fajitas, divide equal amounts of steak and pepper strips, salsa, and cheese onto each of the corn tortillas. Fold up and serve.

MAKE IT A MEAL Complement this dish with a seasonal fruit salad: strawberries and blueberries in summer, and apples and oranges in winter. For dessert, Fried Ice Cream (page 145) is the perfect finishing touch to this Tex-Mex dinner.

Mexican-Style Pizza

FAMILY FAVORITE

SERVES 4

PREP TIME
15 minutes

COOK TIME
20 minutes

PREHEAT
375°F

PER SERVING
Calories: 677
Total fat: 40g
Saturated fat: 17g
Cholesterol: 104mg
Sodium: 1,123mg
Carbohydrates: 46g
Fiber: 9g
Protein: 35g

Pizzas turn out beautifully in the air fryer. This recipe uses premade pizza crusts for ease. You should be able to cook two at a time in most air fryers using a raised rack. The toppings for this pizza are rich and satisfying, including refried beans, frozen meatballs, and salsa.

1¼ cups canned refried beans (from a 15-ounce can)

⅔ cup salsa

1 red bell pepper, chopped

4 (8-inch) focaccia breads or prepared pizza crusts

16 frozen meatballs, thawed and cut in half

1 cup shredded pepper Jack cheese

1 cup shredded Cheddar cheese

½ cup chopped fresh cilantro

1. In a medium bowl, combine the refried beans, salsa, and bell pepper. Spread this mixture on the focaccia breads.

2. Top each pizza with 8 meatball halves, then sprinkle with both cheeses.

3. Set or preheat the air fryer to 375°F. Set 1 pizza in the air fryer basket, add a raised rack and add a second pizza. (If you have a toaster oven-style air fryer you may be able to cook all 4 at once.) Cook for 7 to 10 minutes or until the pizzas are hot and the cheese is starting to brown.

4. Repeat with the remaining 2 pizzas.

5. Sprinkle with the cilantro and serve.

LOVING YOUR LEFTOVERS You can use the rest of the refried beans to make a quesadilla for lunch the next day. Spread a flour or corn tortilla with the beans, then top with some salsa and shredded cheese. Fold in half and cook in the air fryer at 325°F for 5 to 6 minutes, until hot.

Classic Mini Meat Loaves

FAMILY FAVORITE, GLUTEN-FREE

SERVES 4

PREP TIME
15 minutes

COOK TIME
22 minutes

PREHEAT
375°F

PER SERVING
Calories: 321
Total fat: 14g
Saturated fat: 6g
Cholesterol: 134mg
Sodium: 738mg
Carbohydrates: 14g
Fiber: 2g
Protein: 34g

Meat loaf is the classic comfort food. In this recipe, one big meat loaf has been converted to four mini meat loaves. Each little loaf is wrapped in bacon and glazed with a ketchup and mustard mixture. Be sure to have a food thermometer before you cook this recipe.

⅓ **cup quick-cooking oats (gluten-free if needed)**

2 **tablespoons 2% milk**

3 **tablespoons ketchup, divided**

3 **tablespoons Dijon mustard, divided**

1 **large egg**

1 **teaspoon dried marjoram**

¼ **cup grated Parmesan cheese**

½ **teaspoon sea salt**

⅛ **teaspoon freshly ground black pepper**

1 **pound lean ground beef**

4 **bacon slices, uncooked**

1. In a medium bowl, combine the oats, milk, 1 tablespoon of ketchup, 1 tablespoon of mustard, the egg, marjoram, Parmesan, salt, and pepper; mix well. Let stand for 5 minutes.

2. Add the ground beef and mix gently but thoroughly with your hands. Form the beef into four 2-by-5-inch loaves.

3. In a small bowl, combine the remaining 2 tablespoons each of ketchup and mustard.

4. Carefully wrap each mini loaf with the bacon to cover the meat.

5. Set or preheat the air fryer to 375°F. Line the air fryer basket with foil and poke a few holes in the foil. Arrange the meat loaves in the basket. Brush with the ketchup and mustard mixture. Cook the meat loaves for 17 to 22 minutes, testing with a meat thermometer after 17 minutes to see if they have reached 160°F. Continue cooking until they reach that temperature.

MAKE IT A MEAL Serve this classic recipe with Garlicky Green Beans (page 66) and Potatoes au Gratin (page 59), with Carrot Cake (page 157) for dessert.

Savory Lamb Chops

30-MINUTE, FAMILY FAVORITE, GLUTEN-FREE

SERVES 4

PREP TIME
10 minutes

COOK TIME
20 minutes

PREHEAT
375°F

PER SERVING
Calories: 356
Total fat: 16g
Saturated fat: 6g
Cholesterol: 150mg
Sodium: 454mg
Carbohydrates: 8g
Fiber: 1g
Protein: 45g

When cooked in the air fryer, lamb really shines, and its fat content keeps the meat moist and flavorful. Sharp and tart ingredients, such as red currant jelly, cut through the rich flavors and complement the meat's unique qualities.

½ cup chicken broth or stock

2 tablespoons red currant or raspberry jelly

2 tablespoons Dijon mustard

1 tablespoon fresh lemon juice

½ teaspoon dried thyme

8 lamb loin chops (4 to 5 ounces each)

½ teaspoon sea salt

⅛ teaspoon freshly ground black pepper

1. In a small bowl, combine the chicken broth, jelly, mustard, lemon juice, and thyme and mix with a whisk until smooth.

2. Sprinkle the chops with the salt and pepper and brush with some of the broth mixture.

3. Set or preheat the air fryer to 375°F. Arrange 4 chops in a single layer in the air fryer basket. Add a raised rack and top with the remaining chops. (If you don't have a rack, or if they don't fit without overlapping, cook in batches.) Cook the chops for 15 to 20 minutes or until a chop registers at least 145°F on a food thermometer.

4. Put all the chops and the remaining chicken broth mixture in a cake barrel. Put in the air fryer basket and cook for another 3 to 5 minutes or until the sauce is simmering and the chops are tender.

MAKE IT A MEAL   Serve these luscious chops with Roasted Garlic Brussels Sprouts (page 57) and Hasselback Fingerling Potatoes (page 55), with Molten Chocolate Cakes (page 144) for dessert.

Sweet *and* Sour Meat Loaf

FAMILY FAVORITE

SERVES 4

PREP TIME
15 minutes

COOK TIME
30 minutes, plus
10 minutes to stand

PREHEAT
390°F

PER SERVING
Calories: 390
Total fat: 18g
Saturated fat: 7g
Cholesterol: 140mg
Sodium: 582mg
Carbohydrates: 26g
Fiber: 1g
Protein: 31g

Meat loaf is the original comfort food. Most people have a recipe for basic meat loaf, but this one is a bit different. The additions of pineapple juice, brown sugar, and ketchup give it a delicious tang.

¾ pound lean ground beef

½ pound ground pork

⅓ cup soft fresh bread crumbs

4 tablespoons pineapple juice, divided

4 tablespoons light brown sugar, divided

3 tablespoons ketchup, divided

2 tablespoons apple cider vinegar

1 large egg

½ teaspoon sea salt

½ teaspoon onion powder

1. In a large bowl, combine the beef, pork, bread crumbs, 2 tablespoons of pineapple juice, 2 tablespoons of brown sugar, 2 tablespoons of ketchup, the vinegar, egg, salt, and onion powder. Mix gently but thoroughly.

2. Make a foil sling: Tear off 2 (18-inch) lengths of heavy-duty aluminum foil and fold lengthwise into quarters. Place the two strips of foil in an X pattern in the air fryer basket so the edges extend above the basket. Add a parchment paper round with a few holes poked in it to the basket.

3. Set or preheat the air fryer to 390°F. Form the meat loaf mixture into a 7-inch round and gently place in the basket. Fold the foil strips down inside the basket. Cook for 25 minutes.

4. Meanwhile, in a small bowl, combine the remaining 2 tablespoons of pineapple juice, 2 tablespoons of brown sugar, and 1 tablespoon of ketchup and mix.

5. Remove the basket from the air fryer. Glaze the meat loaf with the pineapple juice mixture.

6. Return the basket to the air fryer and cook for another 5 to 10 minutes or until the meat loaf is glazed and reads 160°F on a food thermometer.

7. Use the foil sling to transfer the meat loaf to a serving plate. Cover loosely with foil, let stand for 10 minutes, then slice to serve.

LOVING YOUR LEFTOVERS If you are lucky enough to have any leftover meat loaf, use it to make a meat loaf sandwich the next day. Toast two slices of bread and spread with mayo and ketchup. Top with lettuce, a slice or two of meat loaf, and a sliced tomato. Enjoy.

Steak Bites *and* Mushrooms

SERVES 4

PREP TIME
15 minutes

COOK TIME
15 minutes

PREHEAT
400°F

PER SERVING
Calories: 471
Total fat: 38g
Saturated fat: 19g
Cholesterol: 124mg
Sodium: 460mg
Carbohydrates: 6g
Fiber: 1g
Protein: 29g

Steak bites, or steak tips, as they are sometimes called, are especially tender and juicy when cooked in the air fryer. A buttery garlic sauce and fresh mushrooms add more flavor and texture. Serve this over hot cooked rice to soak up all the delicious sauce.

4 tablespoons (½ stick) butter

1 onion, chopped

8 ounces button mushrooms, halved

2 garlic cloves, minced

1¼ pounds boneless rib-eye or sirloin steak, cut into 1-inch cubes

½ teaspoon sea salt

⅛ teaspoon freshly ground black pepper

2 teaspoons fresh lemon juice

1 teaspoon dried marjoram

2 tablespoons chopped fresh parsley

1. In a cake barrel, combine the butter, onion, mushrooms, garlic, steak cubes, salt, black pepper, lemon juice, marjoram, and parsley.

2. Set or preheat the air fryer to 400°F. Put the cake barrel in the air fryer basket. Cook for 10 to 15 minutes, stirring the food halfway through the cooking time, until the steak registers 145°F on a food thermometer and the vegetables are tender.

INGREDIENT TIP   You want a nice, lean cut of meat for this recipe so it will stay tender during the hot, fast cooking process. Choose steaks that are best for grilling: rib eye, sirloin, porterhouse, New York strip, and T-bone.

Spanish Rice

SERVES 4

PREP TIME
15 minutes

COOK TIME
20 minutes

PREHEAT
375°F

PER SERVING
Calories: 265
Total fat: 4g
Saturated fat: 2g
Cholesterol: 35mg
Sodium: 340mg
Carbohydrates: 41g
Fiber: 4g
Protein: 17g

Spanish rice is a flavorful combination of rice, tomato, ground beef, onions, and spices. This delicious one-pot meal is both comforting and satisfying. You can use either white or brown rice in this easy recipe.

½ **pound lean ground beef**

1 **onion, chopped**

3 **garlic cloves, minced**

2 **(10-ounce) packages frozen white or brown rice, thawed**

1 **tomato, seeded and chopped**

3 **tablespoons tomato paste**

⅔ **cup beef broth or stock**

1 **teaspoon smoked paprika**

½ **teaspoon dried oregano**

½ **teaspoon sea salt**

⅛ **teaspoon freshly ground black pepper**

1. In a cake barrel, combine the ground beef, onion, and garlic. Break up the ground beef with a fork.

2. Set or preheat the air fryer to 375°F. Put the cake barrel in the air fryer basket. Cook for 5 to 7 minutes, stirring halfway through the cooking time, until the ground beef is cooked. Remove the cake barrel and drain if necessary.

3. Add the rice, chopped tomato, tomato paste, beef broth, paprika, oregano, salt, and pepper to the cake barrel and stir. Return the cake barrel to the air fryer basket. Cook for another 8 to 13 minutes, stirring halfway through the cooking time, until the mixture is blended and hot.

SPICE IT UP   This recipe is fairly mild, so add cayenne pepper in place of the black pepper to turn it up a notch. Or, throw in a minced jalapeño along with the onion and garlic. Another option: Add a couple of teaspoons of adobo sauce (from a can of chipotles) when you add the broth.

German Potato Salad

FAMILY FAVORITE, GLUTEN-FREE

SERVES 4

PREP TIME
20 minutes

COOK TIME
30 minutes

PREHEAT
375°F

PER SERVING
Calories: 449
Total fat: 23g
Saturated fat: 8g
Cholesterol: 42mg
Sodium: 546mg
Carbohydrates: 51g
Fiber: 3g
Protein: 11g

German potato salad is a delicious variation on the classic American salad, but with a twist—it's served hot. Potatoes and sausages are mixed in a sweet and sour sauce enriched with sour cream. Though a salad by name, it's also a hearty main dish that will warm you up on a cold day.

2 russet potatoes, peeled and cut into 1-inch cubes

1 cup chicken stock

1 tablespoon olive oil

1 onion, chopped

2 garlic cloves, minced

½ pound fully cooked Polish sausage, sliced

¼ cup apple cider vinegar

3 tablespoons light brown sugar

2 tablespoons cornstarch

¼ cup sour cream

1. In a cake barrel, combine the potatoes and chicken stock. Cover the cake barrel with foil, and poke a few holes in the foil.

2. Set or preheat the air fryer to 375°F. Place the cake barrel in the air fryer basket. Cook the potatoes for 15 to 18 minutes or until they are tender when pierced with a fork.

3. Drain the potatoes in a colander placed in a bowl, reserving the chicken stock.

4. In the cake barrel, combine the olive oil, onion, garlic, and sausage. Return the cake barrel to the air fryer basket. Cook for 4 to 7 minutes or until the onions are crisp-tender and the sausages are hot. Drain if necessary.

5. Add the reserved chicken stock, vinegar, brown sugar, and cornstarch to the mixture in the cake barrel and stir. Cook for another 4 to 6 minutes or until hot.

6. Stir the sour cream into the sauce, then add the potatoes, stirring to coat. Cook for another 2 to 3 minutes or until hot.

MAKE IT A MEAL Serve this dish with Crispy Mushrooms (page 54) and Garlicky Green Beans (page 66). For dessert, make Buckeye Brownies (page 148).

Meatball Taco Pie

FAMILY FAVORITE

SERVES 4

PREP TIME
20 minutes

COOK TIME
20 minutes, plus
10 minutes to cool

PREHEAT
375°F

PER SERVING
Calories: 492
Total fat: 30g
Saturated fat: 15g
Cholesterol: 84mg
Sodium: 921mg
Carbohydrates: 33g
Fiber: 9g
Protein: 27g

A main dish pie is always a nice change of pace, and it's super simple to make a pie in the air fryer. This recipe combines corn tortillas, refried beans, cheese, salsa, and meatballs for a hearty and delicious dinner. You'll need a 7-inch springform pan.

10 frozen meatballs, thawed, cut in half

1 cup salsa

1 cup canned refried beans (from 15-ounce can)

2 teaspoons chili powder

½ teaspoon ground cumin

4 (6-inch) corn tortillas

1 cup shredded pepper Jack cheese

1 cup shredded Colby cheese

1. In a medium bowl, combine the meatball halves, salsa, refried beans, chili powder, and cumin.

2. Put one tortilla in a 7-inch springform pan and top with one-quarter of the meatball mixture. Top with one-quarter of the cheeses. Repeat the layers three more times, ending with cheese.

3. Set or preheat the air fryer to 375°F. Put the springform pan in the air fryer basket and cook for 15 to 20 minutes or until the pie is hot and bubbling and the cheese has melted and started to turn brown on top.

4. Remove the pan from the air fryer and cool on a wire rack for 10 minutes. Run a knife around the edges of the pan and remove the sides of the springform pan, then cut into wedges to serve.

SPICE IT UP To make this recipe spicy, add 1 minced jalapeño pepper to the salsa mixture and increase the chili powder to 1 tablespoon. You can also use all pepper Jack and omit the Colby.

Savory Baby Back Ribs

FAMILY FAVORITE, GLUTEN-FREE

SERVES 4

PREP TIME
10 minutes

COOK TIME
30 minutes

PREHEAT
375°F

PER SERVING
Calories: 282
Total fat: 18g
Saturated fat: 6g
Cholesterol: 75mg
Sodium: 265mg
Carbohydrates: 8g
Fiber: 0g
Protein: 21g

Baby back ribs are also called back ribs or loin ribs. They are called "baby" because they are shorter than spareribs. Cooked in an air fryer, they come out tender and delicious, especially when flavored with this classic American spice mix.

2 tablespoons light brown sugar

2 teaspoons sea salt

1 teaspoon freshly ground black pepper

2 teaspoons onion powder

1 teaspoon garlic powder

1 teaspoon mustard powder

1 teaspoon dried marjoram

4 (4-rib) sections baby back ribs

2 tablespoons barbecue sauce

1. For the seasoning mix: In a small bowl, combine the brown sugar, salt, pepper, onion powder, garlic powder, mustard, and marjoram and mix. Transfer to a small screw-top glass jar. (Some of the seasoning mix is used in this recipe; save the rest for other uses. Store at room temperature.)

2. Rub the ribs with the barbecue sauce and sprinkle with 1 tablespoon of seasoning mix; rub the seasoning all over the ribs.

3. Set or preheat the air fryer to 375°F. Put the ribs in the air fryer basket. Cook for 25 minutes, turning halfway through the cooking time. The ribs should be at least 145°F on a food thermometer.

LOVING YOUR LEFTOVERS Any leftovers from this recipe can be used to make sandwiches. Cut the meat off the bone, then mix with some barbecue sauce and heat in the microwave. Pile onto toasted buns and serve.

Salisbury Steak Burgers

FAMILY FAVORITE

SERVES 4

———————

PREP TIME
15 minutes

———————

COOK TIME
20 minutes

———————

PREHEAT
375°F

———————

PER SERVING
Calories: 321
Total fat: 11g
Saturated fat: 5g
Cholesterol: 78mg
Sodium: 442mg
Carbohydrates: 26g
Fiber: 1g
Protein: 29g

Salisbury steak is mixture of well-seasoned ground beef and cracker crumbs that is cooked in a gravy. Here, in burger form, the patties are flavored with ketchup and Worcestershire and served on toasted onion buns with sautéed mushrooms.

¼ cup cracker crumbs

2 tablespoons beef broth

1 tablespoon ketchup

1 tablespoon Dijon mustard

2 teaspoons Worcestershire sauce

½ teaspoon onion powder

1 pound lean ground beef

1 cup sliced mushrooms

1 tablespoon butter

4 onion buns, split and toasted

1. In a large bowl, combine the cracker crumbs, broth, ketchup, mustard, Worcestershire sauce, and onion powder and mix well. Add the beef and mix gently but thoroughly with your hands. Form into 4 patties and refrigerate while you prepare the mushrooms.

2. In a 6-inch metal pan, combine the mushrooms and butter.

3. Set or preheat the air fryer to 375°F. Put the pan in the air fryer and cook for 8 to 10 minutes, stirring once during the cooking time, until the mushrooms are tender and browned. Remove the pan from the air fryer and set aside.

4. Line the air fryer basket with a round of parchment paper with holes punched into it. Put the burgers in the basket in a single layer. (Depending on the size of your air fryer, you may need to do this in two batches.) Cook the burgers for 11 to 14 minutes or until they register 160°F on a food thermometer.

5. Put the burgers on the onion bun bottoms. Top with the mushrooms, then the bun tops.

MAKE IT A MEAL Serve these burgers with a green salad tossed with mushrooms, bell peppers, and onions, along with Curly Fries (page 36). For dessert, make Lemon Bars (page 154).

Pineapple Pork Kebabs

FAMILY FAVORITE, GLUTEN-FREE

SERVES 4

PREP TIME
15 minutes, plus
30 minutes to soak

COOK TIME
15 minutes

PREHEAT
375°F

PER SERVING
Calories: 267
Total fat: 8g
Saturated fat: 3g
Cholesterol: 76mg
Sodium: 349mg
Carbohydrates: 23g
Fiber: 3g
Protein: 26g

The sweet-tartness of pineapple pairs beautifully with tender and savory pork. These kebabs are fun to make, and even more fun to eat. You can assemble them ahead of time and keep them in the refrigerator until you're ready to cook.

1 pound boneless pork loin chops

½ teaspoon sea salt

⅛ teaspoon freshly ground black pepper

2 (8-ounce) cans juice-packed pineapple chunks, drained, juice reserved

1 green bell pepper, cut into ½-inch chunks

1 red bell pepper, cut into ½-inch chunks

1 tablespoon honey

½ teaspoon ground ginger

1. Soak 8 (6-inch) bamboo skewers in water for 30 minutes.

2. Cut the pork chops into 1½-inch cubes, and sprinkle with the salt and pepper.

3. Thread the pork pieces, pineapple chunks, and bell peppers onto the soaked skewers.

4. In a small bowl, combine 2 tablespoons of the reserved pineapple juice, the honey, and ginger and mix well. Brush this mixture onto the kebabs, using all the mixture.

5. Set or preheat the air fryer to 375°F. Lay 4 of the kebabs in the air fryer basket. Add a raised rack and add the remaining 4 kebabs. (If you don't have a rack, cook them in batches.) Cook for 10 to 14 minutes or until the pork reads 145°F on a food thermometer.

SPICE IT UP To make this recipe hot and spicy, add ¼ teaspoon cayenne pepper to the pineapple juice mixture. You can also add chili powder or ground chiles.

Mongolian Beef

30-MINUTE, GLUTEN-FREE

SERVES 4

PREP TIME
10 minutes

COOK TIME
15 minutes

PREHEAT
400°F

PER SERVING
Calories: 215
Total fat: 6g
Saturated fat: 2g
Cholesterol: 68mg
Sodium: 566mg
Carbohydrates: 14g
Fiber: 0g
Protein: 26g

In this classic Chinese dish, slices of steak are fried until crisp outside and tender inside. They are then coated in a rich sauce made from soy sauce, brown sugar, ginger, and garlic.

1 pound flank steak

4 tablespoons cornstarch, divided

⅛ teaspoon freshly ground black pepper

Cooking oil, for misting

1 tablespoon grated fresh ginger

3 garlic cloves, minced

⅔ cup beef stock

2 tablespoons gluten-free tamari

2 tablespoons light brown sugar

2 scallions, chopped

1. Cut the flank steak against the grain into ½-inch-thick strips. Put in a medium bowl and sprinkle with 3 tablespoons of cornstarch and the pepper; toss to coat.

2. Set or preheat the air fryer to 400°F. Line the air fryer basket with a round of parchment paper that has some holes poked into it. Put the steak in the air fryer basket and mist with cooking oil. Cook the beef for 8 to 12 minutes, shaking the pan after 5 minutes and misting with more cooking oil, until the beef is browned. Remove the beef from the air fryer basket.

3. In a 7-inch metal bowl, combine the remaining 1 tablespoon of cornstarch, the ginger, garlic, beef stock, tamari, brown sugar, and scallions. Place the bowl in the air fryer basket. Cook for 5 to 8 minutes, stirring after 3 minutes, until the sauce thickens and is glossy.

4. Put the beef in a serving dish. Pour the sauce over, toss to coat, and serve.

SPICE IT UP Try adding cayenne pepper or red pepper flakes. You could also mince a serrano pepper and cook it in the sauce.

FRY FACT This recipe is much lower in calories and fat than the typical recipe because the beef doesn't have to be fried in a lot of oil.

Chocolate Chip Pie, page 152

CHAPTER 8

DESSERTS AND BAKED GOODS

Molten Chocolate Cakes

30-MINUTE, FAMILY FAVORITE

SERVES 4

PREP TIME
15 minutes

COOK TIME
12 minutes

PREHEAT
375°F

PER SERVING
Calories: 486
Total fat: 34g
Saturated fat: 20g
Cholesterol: 241mg
Sodium: 230mg
Carbohydrates: 42g
Fiber: 2g
Protein: 6g

Surprise! These cakes have molten chocolate centers. This recipe is perfect for the air fryer: Four small ramekins snuggle right in most air fryer baskets. Serve this treat with cold vanilla ice cream on the side.

⅓ **cup semisweet chocolate chips**

⅓ **cup milk chocolate chips**

7 tablespoons butter, cut into pieces, plus more for the ramekins

⅓ **cup sugar**

1 large egg

3 large egg yolks

¼ **cup all-purpose flour**

Pinch salt

1. In a saucepan over low heat, combine both types of chocolate chips and the butter; cook until the butter melts, stirring until smooth. Stir in the sugar until smooth.

2. Remove the pan from the heat and beat in the whole egg and egg yolks, then beat in the flour and salt until combined.

3. Grease four 4-ounce ramekins with additional unsalted butter. Divide the batter among the cups.

4. Set or preheat the air fryer to 375°F. Put the ramekins in the air fryer basket, leaving some space between them. Cook for 7 to 10 minutes or until the top crust cracks and looks dry.

5. Carefully remove the ramekins (see Tip) from the air fryer basket and let stand for 2 minutes. Then run a knife around the edges of the little cups and unmold them onto serving plates. Serve immediately.

FRY FACT Getting these little ramekins out of the air fryer basket can be tricky. Take your time. Use silicone-tipped tongs or a plate lifter, and remove the ramekins carefully so you don't burn yourself.

Fried Ice Cream

FAMILY FAVORITE, GLUTEN-FREE

SERVES 4

PREP TIME

10 minutes, plus
2 hours to freeze

COOK TIME

2 minutes

PREHEAT

400°F

PER SERVING

Calories: 443
Total fat: 16g
Saturated fat: 8g
Cholesterol: 50mg
Sodium: 235mg
Carbohydrates: 69g
Fiber: 3g
Protein: 10g

Fried ice cream was the "it" restaurant dessert in the 1980s. Although it sounds improbable, you can briefly heat ice cream that's been coated with cereal and frozen. The coating gets crunchy, and the ice cream stays cold. Make this dessert ahead of time, and fry it right before serving.

1½ cups crushed cornflakes

1 cup crushed granola

1 pint ice cream, any flavor

½ cup hot fudge sauce

1. In a shallow bowl, combine the cornflakes and granola. Line a baking sheet with parchment paper.

2. Using a 2-tablespoon ice cream scoop, scoop the ice cream into 8 balls. Dip the ice cream balls in the cereal, turning to coat thoroughly. Make sure you can't see any ice cream through the coating. Put the coated balls on the lined baking sheet and freeze for at least 2 hours or until very firm.

3. When you're ready to eat, line the air fryer basket with heavy-duty aluminum foil.

4. Set or preheat the air fryer to 400°F. Put 3 or 4 frozen ice cream balls on the foil in the air fryer basket. Cook the ice cream for 2 minutes. Don't overcook, or the ice cream will melt.

5. Serve immediately with the hot fudge sauce.

LOVING YOUR LEFTOVERS If your family likes this recipe, make a bunch of the ice cream balls ahead of time. Then you can have fried ice cream any time you want.

Vanilla Wafer Cupcakes

FAMILY FAVORITE

SERVES 4

PREP TIME
20 minutes

COOK TIME
15 minutes, plus
1 hour to cool

PREHEAT
325°F

PER SERVING
Calories: 312
Total fat: 19g
Saturated fat: 7g
Cholesterol: 70mg
Sodium: 189mg
Carbohydrates: 34g
Fiber: 1g
Protein: 3g

These cupcakes come with a surprise: They use crushed vanilla wafers in place of much of the flour. They bake up moist with a strong vanilla flavor. Serve them plain, or top them with a simple vanilla frosting (see Tip).

15 vanilla wafers, finely crushed

2 tablespoons all-purpose flour

¼ teaspoon baking powder

Pinch salt

3 tablespoons butter, melted

¼ cup packed light brown sugar

1 large egg yolk

¼ cup 2% milk

¼ cup chopped pecans

Nonstick baking spray (containing flour)

1. In a medium bowl, combine the wafer crumbs, flour, baking powder, and salt; mix well.

2. In another medium bowl, combine the melted butter, brown sugar, and egg yolk; mix well.

3. Add one-third of the crumb mixture to the butter mixture, beat until smooth, and then add half of the milk. Add another one-third of the crumb mixture and beat. Then add the remaining milk. Finally, beat in the rest of the crumb mixture. Stir in the pecans.

4. Spray 4 silicone muffin cups with baking spray. Divide the batter among the cups.

5. Set or preheat the air fryer to 325°F. Put the filled muffin cups in the air fryer basket. Cook for 13 to 16 minutes or until the cupcakes are golden brown and the centers spring back when gently touched with your finger.

6. Cool for 1 to 1½ hours on a wire rack, then unmold and serve.

SUBSTITUTION TIP To make a frosting for these cupcakes, beat 3 tablespoons of room temperature butter with 1 cup powdered sugar, ½ teaspoon vanilla extract, and 2 to 3 teaspoons of milk.

Peanut Butter Cheesecake Cups

FAMILY FAVORITE

SERVES 6

PREP TIME
20 minutes,
plus time to chill

COOK TIME
35 minutes, plus
1 hour to cool

PREHEAT
325°F

PER SERVING
Calories: 406
Total fat: 25g
Saturated fat: 10g
Cholesterol: 73mg
Sodium: 230mg
Carbohydrates: 39g
Fiber: 2g
Protein: 8g

Mini cheesecakes are fun to make and eat. Start with a chocolate sandwich cookie as a base, flavor the cheesecake batter with peanut butter, and you have a delicious and interesting cheesecake cupcake that everyone will love.

Nonstick baking spray (containing flour)

6 peanut butter–filled chocolate sandwich cookies

3 mini peanut butter cups, cut in half

1 (8-ounce) package cream cheese, at room temperature

¼ cup packed light brown sugar

⅓ cup creamy peanut butter

2 tablespoons buttermilk

1 teaspoon vanilla extract

1 large egg

½ cup hot fudge sauce

1. Spray 6 silicone muffin cups with baking spray.

2. Put one cookie in the bottom of each muffin cup, and top with a peanut butter cup half.

3. In a medium bowl, beat together the cream cheese and brown sugar until smooth. Add the peanut butter, buttermilk, vanilla, and egg and beat until smooth. Spoon over the cookies in each muffin cup, filling three-quarters full.

4. Set or preheat the air fryer to 325°F. Put 3 of the cups in the air fryer basket. Cook for 13 to 17 minutes or until the cheesecakes are just set to the touch.

5. Repeat with remaining cheesecakes. Let all the cheesecakes cool on a wire rack for 1 hour, then refrigerate until chilled.

6. Drizzle with the hot fudge sauce before serving.

INGREDIENT TIP Use the smallest peanut butter cups you can find, or there won't be enough room in the muffin cup for the batter. You could also use a couple of chocolate chips or some candy-coated chocolates in place of the peanut butter cups.

Buckeye Brownies

FAMILY FAVORITE

SERVES 6

PREP TIME
15 minutes

COOK TIME
15 minutes, plus
2 hours to cool

PREHEAT
325°F

PER SERVING
Calories: 548
Total fat: 29g
Saturated fat: 13g
Cholesterol: 54mg
Sodium: 173mg
Carbohydrates: 67g
Fiber: 4g
Protein: 9g

These brownies get their inspiration from buckeye candy, in which all but the top of a peanut butter ball is dipped in chocolate. They are topped with peanut butter frosting and chocolate glaze.

4 tablespoons (½ stick) butter, melted

8 tablespoons creamy peanut butter, divided

⅓ cup granulated sugar

2 tablespoons light brown sugar

1 large egg

1 teaspoon vanilla extract

½ cup all-purpose flour

3 tablespoons unsweetened cocoa powder

Nonstick baking spray (containing flour)

1¼ cups powdered sugar

1 cup semisweet chocolate chips

1. In a medium bowl, combine the melted butter, 2 tablespoons of peanut butter, the granulated sugar, brown sugar, egg, and vanilla; beat well. Stir in the flour and cocoa powder.

2. Coat a 6-by-2-inch round metal pan with baking spray, then add the brownie batter. Cover the pan with foil, crimping the edges to secure. Poke a few holes in the foil with a knife.

3. Set or preheat the air fryer to 325°F. Place the metal pan in the air fryer basket. Bake the brownie for 12 to 16 minutes or until a toothpick inserted near the center comes out with a few crumbs attached.

4. Cool the brownie completely on a wire rack for about 2 hours.

5. In a medium bowl, beat together 4 tablespoons of peanut butter and the powdered sugar; the mixture will be stiff. Spread the frosting over the cooled brownie in an even layer.

6. In a small saucepan, combine the chocolate chips and remaining 2 tablespoons of peanut butter; let the mixture melt over low heat until smooth. Pour this glaze over the brownies; let stand until set.

SUBSTITUTION TIP   You can omit the peanut butter frosting layer in step 5 and stir about ⅓ cup of chopped peanut butter cups into the brownie base. Frost with the chocolate glaze and sprinkle ¼ cup more chopped peanut butter cups on top.

Cracker Candy

FAMILY FAVORITE

SERVES 4

PREP TIME
10 minutes

COOK TIME
4 minutes, plus
45 minutes to cool

PREHEAT
375°F

PER SERVING
Calories: 364
Total fat: 24g
Saturated fat: 13g
Cholesterol: 32mg
Sodium: 160mg
Carbohydrates: 35g
Fiber: 2g
Protein: 3g

Turn the usual cracker candy into an even more irresistible treat by cooking it in an air fryer. In this recipe, the crackers are coated with a toffee mixture, then baked. Chocolate chips and nuts are sprinkled on top. You break the candy into pieces to gobble it up.

Nonstick cooking spray

10 to 12 round buttery crackers

4 tablespoons (½ stick) butter

¼ cup packed light brown sugar

½ cup milk chocolate chips

¼ cup chopped cashews

1. Line a 7-by-2-inch round baking pan with foil, then coat it with cooking spray. Line the bottom with the crackers, breaking some crackers to fill the gaps. You want a single layer of crackers.

2. In a small saucepan, combine the butter and brown sugar; bring to a boil over medium heat, stirring constantly. Boil for 1 minute or until the mixture forms a sauce.

3. Being careful not to burn yourself with the hot sugar, pour the mixture over the crackers in the pan.

4. Set or preheat the air fryer to 375°F. Put the pan in the air fryer basket. Bake the candy for 3 to 5 minutes or until the sauce is bubbling over the entire surface.

5. Remove the pan from the air fryer basket and immediately sprinkle with the chocolate chips. Let stand for a few minutes, then swirl the chocolate over the candy.

6. Sprinkle with the cashews and let stand until cool, about 45 minutes. Remove from the pan and break into pieces to serve.

SUBSTITUTION TIP You can use any kind of cracker you like in this recipe. You can also use semisweet chocolate chips in place of the milk chocolate, and any type of chopped nut.

Bread Pudding Tartlets

FAMILY FAVORITE

SERVES 4

PREP TIME
10 minutes, plus
20 minutes to soak

COOK TIME
10 minutes, plus
20 minutes to cool

PREHEAT
350°F

PER SERVING
Calories: 339
Total fat: 11g
Saturated fat: 6g
Cholesterol: 52mg
Sodium: 188mg
Carbohydrates: 52g
Fiber: 3g
Protein: 7g

A classic comfort food, bread pudding may seem like an unlikely dessert to make in the air fryer. In this recipe, graham cracker tartlet shells cradle the pudding mixture, adding a little crunch to the soft pudding. Serve it with caramel or chocolate sauce drizzled over the top.

⅔ cup whole milk

1 large egg, beaten

¼ cup packed light brown sugar

1 teaspoon vanilla extract

2 slices white sandwich bread, cubed

½ cup semisweet chocolate chips

4 miniature graham cracker tart shells

2 tablespoons demerara sugar or granulated sugar

1. In a medium bowl, stir together the milk, egg, brown sugar, and vanilla. Add the bread cubes and chocolate chips. Let stand for 20 minutes, occasionally pushing the bread down into the liquid so it becomes soaked.

2. Divide the mixture among the graham cracker shells. Sprinkle with the demerara sugar.

3. Set or preheat the air fryer to 350°F. Fit as many little tartlets as you can in the air fryer basket. Cook for 10 to 12 minutes or until the puddings are set and golden brown on top.

4. Repeat with remaining shells if necessary. Let cool for 20 minutes, then serve.

SUBSTITUTION TIP You can add just about anything to these little bread pudding tartlets. Use milk chocolate chips in place of the semisweet chocolate, substitute dried cranberries for the chocolate, or use some chopped toasted nuts.

Baklava Twist *with* Mixed Nuts

FAMILY FAVORITE

SERVES 6

PREP TIME
25 minutes

COOK TIME
20 minutes, plus
2 hours to cool

PREHEAT
375°F

PER SERVING
Calories: 344
Total fat: 24g
Saturated fat: 8g
Cholesterol: 27mg
Sodium: 145mg
Carbohydrates: 34g
Fiber: 3g
Protein: 3g

Baklava is made with layered phyllo dough, sugar and nuts, and a honey syrup. In this recipe, the dough is rolled in the pan before baking.

½ cup packed light brown sugar

2 teaspoons ground cinnamon

1 teaspoon ground nutmeg

½ teaspoon ground cardamom or ginger

4 (9-by-15-inch) sheets frozen phyllo dough, thawed

⅓ cup butter, melted

1 cup finely chopped mixed nuts, divided

Nonstick baking spray (containing flour)

⅓ cup honey

1. For the spice mix: In a small bowl, mix together the brown sugar, cinnamon, nutmeg, and cardamom. Transfer to a small glass screw-top jar. (Some of the spice mix is used in this recipe; save the rest for other uses. Store at room temperature.)

2. Place one of the thawed sheets of phyllo dough on a work surface. Brush with about 1 tablespoon of melted butter, then add a second sheet of phyllo. Sprinkle with ½ cup nuts and 2 tablespoons of the spice mix. Starting with a long side, roll up the phyllo, enclosing the nut mixture, brushing with butter as you work.

3. Spray a 6-by-2-inch metal pan with baking spray. Starting at the outside, coil the phyllo roll in the pan.

4. Repeat with the remaining phyllo sheets and the remaining ½ cup nuts and 2 tablespoons spice mix. Continue to coil the phyllo roll in the same pan, working in toward the center. Be gentle so you don't crack the roll. Drizzle any remaining butter on top.

5. Set or preheat the air fryer to 375°F. Place the pan in the air fryer basket. Bake the twist for 15 to 20 minutes or until golden and crisp.

6. Remove the pan from the air fryer and immediately drizzle it with the honey in a slow stream. Let cool for about 2 hours, then cut into wedges to serve.

Chocolate Chip Pie

FAMILY FAVORITE

SERVES 6

PREP TIME
20 minutes

COOK TIME
30 minutes, plus
30 minutes to cool

PREHEAT
350°F

PER SERVING
Calories: 560
Total fat: 30g
Saturated fat: 15g
Cholesterol: 121mg
Sodium: 320mg
Carbohydrates: 69g
Fiber: 2.5g
Protein: 7g

Put a chocolate chip cookie in a pie crust, and you get this rich, decadent pie. It's perfect with a scoop of vanilla or chocolate chip cookie dough ice cream melting on top. You'll need a 7-inch springform pan.

⅓ **cup butter**

½ **cup packed light brown sugar**

⅓ **cup light corn syrup**

2 large eggs

1 large egg yolk

1 teaspoon vanilla extract

⅓ **cup all-purpose flour**

1 cup semisweet chocolate chips

1 store-bought refrigerated pie crust

1. In a medium saucepan, melt the butter over medium heat. Remove the pan from the heat and stir in the brown sugar and corn syrup, mixing well.

2. Add the whole eggs and egg yolk and beat. Then add the vanilla and the flour. Finally, stir in the chocolate chips.

3. Line a 7-inch springform pan with the premade pie crust, easing it into the pan. Do not stretch the pie crust. Trim the top edge of the crust off so it's even with the top of the pan, then fold down the top ½ inch and flute.

4. Pour the filling into the pan.

5. Set or preheat the air fryer to 350°F. Place the pan in the air fryer basket. Bake for 25 to 30 minutes or until the pie is set. If the top is browning too much before the pie is set, cover it with foil.

6. Let the pie cool for 30 minutes, then run a knife around the edge of the pie and remove the sides. Cut into wedges to serve.

SUBSTITUTION TIP Instead of the semisweet chocolate chips, you could add a cup of chopped cashews, or milk chocolate chips, or even some finely chopped candy bars.

Mini Cashew Chocolate Tartlets

FAMILY FAVORITE

SERVES 4

PREP TIME
20 minutes

COOK TIME
12 minutes, plus
1 hour to cool

PREHEAT
300°F

PER SERVING
Calories: 386
Total fat: 22g
Saturated fat: 10g
Cholesterol: 17mg
Sodium: 154mg
Carbohydrates: 44g
Fiber: 2g
Protein: 5g

Mini phyllo shells are found in the frozen foods section of the supermarket. They are a great shortcut when making anything from appetizers to desserts. In this case, they are filled with a rich mixture of brown sugar, cashews, and chocolate. Figure three to four tartlets per person.

3 tablespoons light brown sugar

2 tablespoons butter, melted

2 tablespoons light corn syrup

1 teaspoon vanilla extract

½ cup chopped salted cashews

½ cup mini semisweet chocolate chips, divided

15 mini frozen phyllo shells

1. In a small bowl, combine the brown sugar, melted butter, corn syrup, and vanilla and mix well.

2. Divide the cashews and ¼ cup of chocolate chips among the phyllo shells.

3. Carefully and slowly spoon the brown sugar mixture into the shells on top of the nuts and chocolate chips, filling each almost to the top.

4. Place 7 or 8 of the little shells on the bottom of 7-inch springform pan or a 7-inch round baking sheet.

5. Set or preheat the air fryer to 300°F. Place the pan in the air fryer basket. Bake the tartlets for 4 to 6 minutes or until the filling is bubbling. Remove from the air fryer and cool for about 1 hour on a wire rack. Repeat with remaining tartlets.

6. In a small microwave-safe bowl, melt the remaining ¼ cup chocolate chips on medium power for about 30 seconds, then stir until smooth. Drizzle this mixture on the tartlets. Let stand until set, then serve.

INGREDIENT TIP You don't need to thaw the phyllo shells before preparing; they thaw in seconds in the air fryer.

Lemon Bars

FAMILY FAVORITE

SERVES 6

PREP TIME
20 minutes

COOK TIME
25 minutes, plus
3 hours to cool
and chill

PREHEAT
325°F

PER SERVING
Calories: 341
Total fat: 12g
Saturated fat: 7g
Cholesterol: 118mg
Sodium: 114mg
Carbohydrates: 54g
Fiber: 1g
Protein: 5g

There's just something irresistible about lemon bars and their combination of smooth and creamy lemon filling with crisp crust. This recipe gets crunch from crushed lemon candies that are sprinkled on top.

¾ cup all-purpose flour, plus 2 tablespoons

3 tablespoons powdered sugar

5 tablespoons butter, melted

3 large eggs

1 cup granulated sugar

6 tablespoons fresh lemon juice

4 hard lemon candies, crushed

1. In a medium bowl, combine ¾ cup of flour and the powdered sugar and mix well. Stir in the melted butter until crumbly.

2. Press this mixture into the bottom of a 6-by-2-inch round metal pan.

3. Set or preheat the air fryer to 325°F. Place the pan in the air fryer basket. Bake the crust for 5 to 7 minutes or until just set. Remove from the basket.

4. In a medium bowl, with a hand mixer, beat the eggs until foamy. Gradually add the granulated sugar, beating constantly, until the mixture is fluffy and light yellow, about 5 minutes. Add the remaining 2 tablespoons of flour and mix well. Stir the lemon juice into the egg mixture, then pour the mixture over the crust.

5. Return the pan to the air fryer and bake for 10 minutes or until just barely set. Carefully remove the basket from the air fryer and sprinkle the candies over the top.

6. Return to the air fryer and bake for another 5 to 10 minutes or until the topping is set.

7. Let cool on a wire rack for 1 hour, then refrigerate for about 2 hours, until the bar is cold. Cut into wedges to serve. Store, covered, in the refrigerator up to 3 days.

INGREDIENT TIP Before juicing, roll the lemon on the counter under your palm, pressing down firmly, until the lemon softens slightly. Alternatively, pierce it with a fork and microwave for 10 to 30 seconds on high.

Baked Stuffed Apples

FAMILY FAVORITE, GLUTEN-FREE

SERVES 4

PREP TIME
15 minutes

COOK TIME
20 minutes, plus
20 minutes to cool

PREHEAT
350°F

PER SERVING
Calories: 410
Total fat: 20g
Saturated fat: 9g
Cholesterol: 31mg
Sodium: 101mg
Carbohydrates: 61g
Fiber: 6g
Protein: 3g

Stuffed apples are an old-fashioned comfort food that fits the bill when you're looking for a fruit-forward treat. The filling is made from cashews and dried cranberries with a bit of sugar. The scent of these baking apples will fill your home with the flavors of fall.

4 apples

1 tablespoon fresh lemon juice

½ cup coarsely chopped cashews

½ cup dried cranberries

¼ cup packed light brown sugar

4 tablespoons (½ stick) butter, at room temperature

½ teaspoon ground cinnamon

½ cup apple juice

1. Core the apples from the top, being careful not to cut through the bottom. To prevent splitting, peel a strip of skin from each apple around the top of the cored section. Brush the peeled areas with the lemon juice.

2. In a small bowl, combine the cashews, cranberries, brown sugar, butter, and cinnamon; mix well. Stuff this mixture into the apples, heaping it up on top.

3. Put the apples in a 7-by-2-inch round metal pan. Pour the apple juice into the bottom of the pan.

4. Set or preheat the air fryer to 350°F. Place the pan in the air fryer basket. Cook for 15 to 20 minutes or until the apples are tender when pierced with a fork. Cool for 20 minutes, then serve.

INGREDIENT TIP   Some apples are better for baking than others. For this recipe, you want an apple that will hold its shape during baking. Choose Granny Smith, Jonathan, Honeycrisp, Winesap, Northern Spy, or Gala apples.

Carrot Cake

SERVES 6

PREP TIME
20 minutes

COOK TIME
30 minutes, plus
2 hours to cool

PREHEAT
325°F

PER SERVING
Calories: 620
Total fat: 31g
Saturated fat: 19g
Cholesterol: 144mg
Sodium: 286mg
Carbohydrates: 79g
Fiber: 1g
Protein: 7g

This carrot cake is just plain indulgent. Baked to perfection in a cake barrel, it's then frosted with luscious cream cheese frosting. One trick to the best carrot cake is to use baby carrots. They are more tender than large carrots—and sweeter, too.

1¾ cups all-purpose flour

¾ cup packed light
brown sugar

1 teaspoon baking powder

½ teaspoon ground cinnamon

2 large eggs

2 tablespoons apple juice

¾ cup shredded baby carrots
(about 12 carrots)

12 tablespoons (1½ sticks)
butter, 8 tablespoons melted,
4 tablespoons at
room temperature

Nonstick baking spray
(containing flour)

4 ounces cream cheese

1⅓ cups powdered sugar

1. In a large bowl, combine the flour, brown sugar, baking powder, and cinnamon; mix well. Add the eggs, apple juice, and baby carrots; mix until everything is evenly incorporated.

2. Coat a cake barrel with baking spray and pour in the batter.

3. Set or preheat the air fryer to 325°F. Place the cake barrel in the air fryer basket. Bake the cake for 30 minutes or until a toothpick inserted in the center of the cake comes out clean. Let cool on a wire rack for 2 hours.

4. For the frosting, beat the remaining 4 tablespoons (½ stick) of room-temperature butter with the cream cheese until smooth. Beat in the powdered sugar until smooth. Frost the cooled cake. Cut into wedges to serve.

INGREDIENT TIP When you measure flour, always spoon the flour into the measuring cup until it's heaping, then level it off with the back of a knife. Never scoop the measuring cup into the flour, because you'll end up with too much flour.

Pound Cake Bites *with* Cinnamon Dip

SERVES 6

PREP TIME
10 minutes

COOK TIME
8 minutes

PREHEAT
350°F

PER SERVING
Calories: 425
Total fat: 18g
Saturated fat: 8g
Cholesterol: 27mg
Sodium: 328mg
Carbohydrates: 61g
Fiber: 1g
Protein: 6g

This easy, delicious dessert is especially appealing to children, who love dipping and desserts. In fact, they may want to help you make this recipe, in which little cubes of pound cake are coated in cinnamon sugar and air-fried until crisp. The accompanying sweet cinnamon dip is a treat.

1 (16-ounce) frozen pound cake, thawed

⅓ cup sugar

1½ teaspoons ground cinnamon, divided

4 tablespoons (½ stick) butter, melted

1 cup vanilla Greek yogurt

3 tablespoons packed light brown sugar

½ teaspoon vanilla extract

1. Cut the pound cake into 1-inch cubes. If any of the crust comes off, discard (or eat) it. In a shallow bowl, combine the sugar and 1 teaspoon of cinnamon.

2. Drizzle the cake cubes with the melted butter, then place them in the shallow bowl with the sugar mixture and toss until coated.

3. Set or preheat the air fryer to 350°F. Place as many cubes as will fit in a single layer in the air fryer basket. Cook the cubes for 3 to 4 minutes or until golden. Remove the cake cubes from the air fryer and place on a serving plate.

4. Repeat with a second batch.

5. Meanwhile, in a small bowl, combine the yogurt, brown sugar, remaining ½ teaspoon of cinnamon, and the vanilla; mix well.

6. When all the cubes are done, serve them with the dip.

SPICE IT UP Don't limit yourself to cinnamon in this recipe. Think about adding a bit of nutmeg or cardamom. Or if you like spice, a pinch cayenne pepper mixed with the sugar will add some kick.

Roasted Pear Tart

SERVES 6

PREP TIME
20 minutes

COOK TIME
30 minutes, plus
1 hour to cool

PREHEAT
350°F

PER SERVING
Calories: 203
Total fat: 8g
Saturated fat: 2g
Cholesterol: 0mg
Sodium: 198mg
Carbohydrates: 31g
Fiber: 2g
Protein: 2g

Pears are the perfect fruit to bake into a tart. This simple recipe highlights the pears' bright flavor. Serve this tart with vanilla ice cream, and drizzle caramel sauce over the top.

1 store-bought refrigerated pie crust

2 pears

1 teaspoon fresh lemon juice

2 tablespoons light brown sugar

1 tablespoon cornstarch

¼ teaspoon ground nutmeg

2 tablespoons apple jelly

1. Fit the pie crust into a 7-inch springform pan, easing it down into the pan, then pressing it into the bottom and up the sides. Trim the edges of the crust so they are even with the top of the pan. Then, fold down about ¾ inch of the crust from the top, and use your fingers to flute it. Refrigerate the crust while you prepare the filing.

2. Peel the pears, core them, and cut them into ¼-inch slices. Put the pear slices in a medium bowl and sprinkle with the lemon juice. Add the brown sugar, cornstarch, and nutmeg and toss.

3. Arrange the pear slices in the pie crust in a circular fashion.

4. Set or preheat the air fryer to 350°F. Place the springform pan in the air fryer basket. Bake the pie for 25 to 35 minutes or until the crust is golden brown and the pears are tender. Cover with foil for the last 10 minutes if the crust is browning too quickly.

5. Remove the tart from the air fryer, and place it on a wire rack.

6. In a small saucepan, melt the apple jelly over low heat. Drizzle over the pears. Cool the tart for 1 hour, then cut into wedges to serve.

INGREDIENT TIP   There are several types of premade pie crusts on the market, including frozen versions and the refrigerated type that is sold rolled-up. You want the refrigerated, rolled-up version for this recipe. Or, you can make your own crust.

FRY TIMES

These two charts are handy cheat sheets for air frying the most common fresh and frozen foods. This is useful when you just want to make French fries or fry some frozen chicken nuggets without any other ingredients. You'll find cooking times by quantity, the optimum air fryer temperatures, and tips on how to prepare the foods properly for this appliance. Learn how to cook raw and frozen meats, such as poultry, bacon, sausages, and steak. Get tips on preparing raw and frozen veggies such as cauliflower, green beans,

Fry Time: Fresh Foods

Food Name	Quantity	Time
Asparagus	1 pound	5 to 6 minutes, shaking basket halfway
Bacon	6 slices	5 to 8 minutes, turning with tongs halfway, until crisp
Beef, burger	4 patties (4 ounces each)	12 to 17 minutes, turning halfway. Cook to 160°F internal temp
Beef, steak	3 filets, Porterhouse, rib eye, or T-bone (8 ounces each)	18 to 23 minutes, flipping halfway. Cook to 145°F internal temp
Bell peppers	3 peppers	10 minutes, shaking basket halfway
Broccoli and cauliflower	1 pound florets	8 minutes, shaking basket halfway
Chicken, breasts	4 boneless breasts (6 ounces each) 3 bone-in breasts (8 ounces each)	15 to 20 minutes for boneless, flipping halfway. 25 to 30 for bone-in, flipping halfway. Cook to 165°F internal temp
Chicken, tenders	1 pound	15 to 20 minutes, flipping halfway. Cook to 165°F internal temp

broccoli, and potato wedges. And learn how to make convenience foods such as frozen pot stickers, chicken fingers, and mozzarella sticks in the air fryer. Additionally, get tips on how to spice things up by using just a few simple ingredients such as herbs, cheeses, or oils for more flavor. Remember to always use a food thermometer when you are cooking meats, whether from fresh or frozen.

Temperature	Tips	Spice It Up
400°F	Rinse well and cut into 2-inch segments	Drizzle with lime juice and sprinkle with Aleppo pepper
400°F	Place in a single layer in basket	Sprinkle with brown sugar and red pepper flakes before cooking
375°F	Handle beef gently. Press a divot in the center so the burgers don't puff while cooking	Mix in cracker crumbs, salt, pepper, ketchup, and mustard powder. Top with cheese, guacamole, or salad dressing after
400°F	Trim off excess fat, leaving about ¼ inch on each steak	Rub with steak sauce or barbecue sauce before cooking, or sprinkle with dried herbs, salt, and pepper
400°F	Cut into ½-inch strips	Sprinkle with a mixture of dried thyme and basil leaves
400°F	Make sure florets are about the same size	Drizzle with lemon juice, sprinkle with salt and pepper
375°F	Trim off excess fat before cooking	Rub with barbecue sauce before cooking, or sprinkle with fresh herbs after
375°F	Pull off the tendon that can run down the side before cooking	Dip in beaten egg, then in cracker or cereal crumbs seasoned with dried herbs

Food Name	Quantity	Time
Chicken, thighs	4 to 6 boneless thighs 4 to 6 bone-in thighs	20 minutes for boneless 25 minutes for bone-in Cook to 165°F internal temp
Chicken, wings	2 pounds	22 to 25 minutes, shaking basket halfway Cook to 165°F internal temp
Fish, fillets	4 fillets (6 ounces each)	10 to 12 minutes, flipping halfway, until the fillets flake
Meatballs	1 pound (1-inch) meatballs	8 to 12 minutes, turning halfway Cook to 160°F internal temp
Pork, chops	2 bone-in chops (1 inch thick) 3 boneless chops (1 inch thick)	12 to 15 minutes for bone-in and boneless, flipping halfway Cook to 145°F internal temp with a 3-minute stand time
Pork, tenderloin	1- to 1¼-pound	15 to 20 minutes Cook to 145°F internal temp with a 3-minute stand time
Potato, baked	2 or 3 potatoes (about 8 ounces each)	40 to 45 minutes
Potatoes, small	1 pound creamer or baby potatoes	15 to 20 minutes, shaking basket halfway
Potato, wedges	12 wedges, peeled or not	15 to 20 minutes, flipping halfway
Salmon	4 fillets (6 ounces each) 3 steaks (8 ounces each)	7 to 9 minutes for fillets, 17 to 19 minutes for steaks Cook to 145°F internal temp
Shrimp	1 pound medium shrimp	7 to 9 minutes, shaking basket halfway, until curled and pink

Temperature	Tips	Spice It Up
375°F	Trim off excess fat before cooking. Pound to ½-inch thickness for 5 to 10 minutes less cooking time	Rub with mixture of mustard powder and onion powder before cooking, or brush with ranch dressing
375°F	Cut wings into drumettes, flats, and tips; discard tips	Coat in egg and flour mixed with grated Parmesan cheese
350°F	Spray the fish with cooking oil on both sides	Sprinkle with Old Bay seasoning, dredge in egg, roll in cracker crumbs
375°F	Chill meatballs for 2 hours before cooking so they keep their shape	Serve in pasta sauce or with barbecue sauce or blue cheese dressing for dipping
400°F	Trim off excess fat before cooking	Rub the chops with mustard and brown sugar before cooking
375°F	Pull off outer silverskin if attached, or ask butcher to do this	Cut slits in meat and insert garlic slivers. Rub with dried herbs
400°F	Rub the potato skins with olive and prick with a fork before baking	Split and top with sour cream, bacon bits, shredded cheese, and scallions
400°F	Cut in half to cook in 10 minutes	Sprinkle with grated Parmesan or Romano cheese
400°F	Cut each potato into 12 wedges	Drizzle with melted butter and sprinkle with any grated cheese
375°F	Run your finger over the fish to check for small bones; remove with tweezers	Sprinkle with salt, pepper, and herbs before frying, and drizzle with lemon juice after frying
350°F	Make sure shrimp is deveined. You can leave the tails on	Sprinkle with lemon juice, paprika, and lemon pepper before cooking

Fry Time: Frozen Foods

Food Name	Quantity	Time
Burritos	3 to 4 burritos	25 to 35 minutes, flipping halfway
Chicken fingers	10 to 12 pieces	12 to 15 minutes, flipping halfway Cook to 165°F internal temp
Chicken nuggets	15 to 20 pieces	10 to 15 minutes
Corn dogs	4 to 6	8 to 12 minutes, flipping halfway
Egg rolls	1 pound	12 to 16 minutes, flipping halfway, until crisp and hot
Fish sticks	10 to 12 pieces	9 to 12 minutes, flipping halfway and adding more oil
Fish fillets	4 to 6 pieces	10 to 12 minutes, flipping halfway
Fries, steak	1 pound	15 to 18 minutes, shaking basket halfway
Fries, thin	Up to 1 pound	8 to 10 minutes, shaking basket halfway
Hash brown patties	4 to 6 patties	8 to 12 minutes, flipping halfway
Mozzarella sticks	8 to 10	4 to 7 minutes, flipping after 3 minutes

Temperature	Tips	Spice It Up
375°F	Brush with oil before cooking	Serve with salsa or guacamole
400°F	Put in basket in a single layer. Mist with cooking oil. Look for fingers made with real whole chicken breast, not chopped chicken	Serve with a sauce made of mayonnaise and honey mustard
400°F	Choose nuggets that are made with real chicken breast and few additives	Serve with a sauce made of mayo, mustard, and dried thyme
350°F	Watch out for the stick, which will get hot. Use paper towel to hold the sticks while eating	Serve with ketchup or mustard, or a mix of both
350°F	For a crisp crust, brush with slightly beaten egg white before cooking and again halfway through cooking	Serve with a sauce made from ketchup, soy sauce, lemon juice, and honey
375°F	Arrange in a single layer, don't overlap; mist with cooking oil	Sprinkle the fish with smoked paprika and chili powder before cooking
400°F	Choose beer-battered fillets, and look for wild-caught for the best flavor	Sprinkle fillets with grated Parmesan cheese when you flip them
400°F	Arrange in a single layer in the basket, and spray with oil	Sprinkle with chili powder and cumin after cooking
400°F	Spray with oil	Before cooking, sprinkle with smoked paprika
400°F	Put in a single layer. Mist with cooking oil before cooking and again halfway through cooking	Serve with dipping sauce made of sour cream and Russian dressing
350°F	Put in basket in a single layer, and mist with cooking oil before cooking and again halfway through cooking	Sprinkle with paprika, chili powder, or cayenne pepper before cooking. Serve with hot marinara sauce for dipping

Food Name	Quantity	Time
Onion rings	1 pound	8 to 10 minutes, flipping halfway
Pot stickers	6 to 8	13 to 17 minutes, flipping halfway
Sausage links	8 to 10 breakfast sausages 4 to 6 Italian sausage links	12 to 17 minutes for breakfast sausage, flipping halfway 20 to 25 for Italian sausage, flipping halfway Cook to 160°F internal temp
Sausage patties	6 to 8 patties	15 to 20 minutes Cook to 160°F internal temp
Shrimp	1 pound (breaded or not)	12 to 14 minutes, shaking basket halfway
Tater Tots	12 to 16 tots	10 to 13 minutes, shaking basket halfway
Vegetables	12 to 16 pieces	12 to 17 minutes for tender vegetables 20 to 25 for firm vegetables, such as winter squash
Waffle fries	1 pound	8 to 10 minutes, shaking basket halfway

Temperature	Tips	Spice It Up
400°F	Look for onion rings made with whole onions. Mist with oil before cooking and again halfway through cooking	Serve with a dipping sauce made from apple jelly and mustard
350°F	Put in a single layer. Brush with olive oil before cooking and again halfway through cooking	Sprinkle with chili powder or cayenne pepper before cooking
350°F	Line the basket with a round of parchment paper	Serve with raspberry jelly or ranch salad dressing for dipping
400°F	Leave some space around the patties. Be careful of hot fat left in the basket	Sprinkle with smoked paprika before cooking. Serve with cocktail sauce or ketchup.
375°F	Look for Gulf shrimp for the best flavor	Serve with cocktail sauce mixed with cream cheese
350°F	Put in basket in single layer	Serve with ketchup or mustard or mayonnaise
375°F	Don't crowd in the basket, and place in single layer for best results to let water evaporate	Sprinkle with lemon juice and red pepper flakes after cooking
375°F	Mist with cooking oil before cooking and again halfway through cooking	Sprinkle with seasoned salt or celery salt before cooking

MEASUREMENT CONVERSIONS

VOLUME EQUIVALENTS (LIQUID)

US Standard	US Standard (ounces)	Metric (approximate)
2 tablespoons	1 fl. oz.	30 mL
¼ cup	2 fl. oz.	60 mL
½ cup	4 fl. oz.	120 mL
1 cup	8 fl. oz.	240 mL
1½ cups	12 fl. oz.	355 mL
2 cups or 1 pint	16 fl. oz.	475 mL
4 cups or 1 quart	32 fl. oz.	1 L
1 gallon	128 fl. oz.	4 L

OVEN TEMPERATURES

Fahrenheit (F)	Celsius (C) (approximate)
250°F	120°C
300°F	150°C
325°F	165°C
350°F	180°C
375°F	190°C
400°F	200°C
425°F	220°C
450°F	230°C

VOLUME EQUIVALENTS (DRY)

US Standard	Metric (approximate)
⅛ teaspoon	0.5 mL
¼ teaspoon	1 mL
½ teaspoon	2 mL
¾ teaspoon	4 mL
1 teaspoon	5 mL
1 tablespoon	15 mL
¼ cup	59 mL
⅓ cup	79 mL
½ cup	118 mL
⅔ cup	156 mL
¾ cup	177 mL
1 cup	235 mL
2 cups or 1 pint	475 mL
3 cups	700 mL
4 cups or 1 quart	1 L

WEIGHT EQUIVALENTS

US Standard	Metric (approximate)
½ ounce	15 g
1 ounce	30 g
2 ounces	60 g
4 ounces	115 g
8 ounces	225 g
12 ounces	340 g
16 ounces or 1 pound	455 g

INDEX

C

G

ABOUT THE AUTHOR

 **LINDA LARSEN** is an author and home economist who has been developing recipes for years. As the author of the Busy Cook's Guide at About.com for 15 years, she wrote about food safety and quick cooking. She has written 44 cookbooks, including *The Complete Air Fryer Cookbook, The Complete Slow Cooking for Two,* and *Eating Clean for Dummies.* Linda has worked for the Pillsbury Company since 1988, creating and testing recipes and working for the Pillsbury Bake-Off. She holds a bachelor of arts degree in biology from St. Olaf College and a bachelor of science degree with high distinction in food science and nutrition from the University of Minnesota. She lives in Minnesota with her husband.

CPSIA information can be obtained
at www.ICGtesting.com
Printed in the USA
JSHW032355030820
7106JS00003B/4